Knowledge and Censorship

Knowledge and Censorship

Ilan Stavans
with
Verónica Albin

KNOWLEDGE AND CENSORSHIP
Copyright © Ilan Stavans, 2008.
Softcover reprint of the hardcover 1st edition 2008 978-1-4039-8410-4

First published in 2008 by
PALGRAVE MACMILLAN™
175 Fifth Avenue, New York, N.Y. 10010 and
Houndmills, Basingstoke, Hampshire, England RG21 6XS
Companies and representatives throughout the world.

PALGRAVE MACMILLAN is the global academic imprint of the Palgrave Macmillan division of St. Martin's Press, LLC and of Palgrave Macmillan Ltd. Macmillan® is a registered trademark in the United States, United Kingdom and other countries. Palgrave is a registered trademark in the European Union and other countries.

ISBN 978-1-349-53962-8   ISBN 978-0-230-61125-2 (eBook)
DOI 10.1057/9780230611252

Library of Congress Cataloging-in-Publication Data

Stavans, Ilan.
     Knowledge and censorship / Ilan Stavans ; with Verónica Albin.
       p. cm.
     Includes bibliographical references and index.
       1. Stavans, Ilan—Interviews. I. Albin, Verónica, 1955– II. Title.

PS3619.T385K58 2008
864'.64—dc22   2007039394

A catalogue record for this book is available from the British Library.

Design by Newgen Imaging Systems (P) Ltd., Chennai, India.

First edition: April 2008

10 9 8 7 6 5 4 3 2 1

Transferred to Digital Printing in 2013

Also by Ilan Stavans

Fiction
The Disappearance
The One-Handed Pianist and Other Stories

Nonfiction
Love and Language (with Verónica Albin)
The Riddle of Cantinflas
Dictionary Days
On Borrowed Words
Spanglish
The Hispanic Condition
Art and Anger
The Inveterate Dreamer
Octavio Paz: A Meditation
Imagining Columbus
Bandido
¡Lotería! (with Teresa Villegas)

Anthologies
Lengua Fresca (with Harold Augenbraum)
Tropical Synagogues
The Schocken Book of Modern Sephardic Literature
Wáchale!
The Scroll and the Cross
The Oxford Book of Jewish Stories
Mutual Impressions
The Oxford Book of Latin American Essays
Growing Up Latino (with Harold Augenbraum)

Cartoons
Latino USA (with Lalo López Alcaráz)

Translations
Sentimental Songs, by Felipe Alfau

Editions

César Vallejo: Spain, Take This Chalice from Me
The Poetry of Pablo Neruda
Encyclopedia Latina (four volumes)
I Explain a Few Things
The Collected Stories of Calvert Casey
Cesar Chavez: An Organizer's Tale
Rubén Darío: Selected Writings
Isaac Bashevis Singer: Collected Stories (three volumes)

General

The Essential Ilan Stavans
Ilan Stavans: Eight Conversations (with Neal Sokol)
Collins Q&A: Latino Literature and Culture
Conversations with Ilan Stavans

Information is the currency of democracy.
—Thomas Jefferson

CONTENTS

PREFACE

In the fall of 2006 Gabriella Georgiades, known as Ella among friends, the humanities editor at Palgrave Macmillan in New York, envisioned including between two covers three interviews I made with Ilan Stavans. They revolved around the provocative topics of language, translation, silence, and censorship. She contemplated a fourth dialogue devoted to knowledge, thus rounding out the concept of how humans acquire and disseminate information. In addition, she suggested supplementing these four interviews with four brief, first-person meditations she read by Stavans, which were unified by a single motif: the quest for individual freedom in society, especially as it pertains to freedom of speech, belief, and action.

In the preface to *Love and Language* (Yale University Press, 2007), I describe how I first met Stavans at a conference of the American Translators Association in Toronto, where he was delivering the Marilyn Gaddis Rose lecture. To what I've already said in that preface, I would like to add that I became interested in Stavans in part because he is still very much the urchin from Copilco we saw in *On Borrowed Words*. To this day, Stavans crosses the street where he shouldn't, plays with his food, and changes the rules of the game when you least expect it. But you can't really spank him—or at least not every time—because somehow, without anyone noticing, he often manages to make a point no one else had yet made. Stavans is a bit of an imp and that pixyish attitude makes exploring the world of ideas with him a great deal of fun. When you travel with him, you trade the comfort of an Ivory Tower office for an uncertain perch on that precarious aerie on the topmast of some caravel, dizzy with the knowledge that he's already thrown the charts overboard and you may very well get blown off the map. But let me expand on the inception of *Knowledge and Censorship*. Stavans and I got together for dinner in Houston in November 2004 without knowing each other well at all. While the hors d'oeuvre was being served, I realized that we were both hooked on dictionaries, each owning several hundred and each having authored one, and written and lectured extensively on them both formally and informally. By the time dessert came around, we agreed in that the dictionary is the embodiment of knowledge just as much as it is an instrument of censorship. In other words, there could not be a meaningful discussion of lexicons without a thorough exploration of the flow, and interruption, of information.

As soon as I embarked on this first interview with Stavans, I knew I had a book in hand. That book—it turned out to be two plus a chapter on language and empire for Vanderbilt University Press—would revolve around freedom, identity, ethnicity, and knowledge. I got down to work immediately and was in constant touch via phone, fax, snail mail, and e-mail. Stavans and I talked to friend and foe all over the world, we picked our students' brains, we read and surfed voraciously, and exchanged not only books and scholarly

papers but also off-the-wall URLs, trivia, and cultural tidbits
we remembered from our having grown up in Mexico City
in the 1960s. We met in person as often as our schedules
allowed. We made it a point to do so in cities we knew well
(New York, Amherst, Houston, Mexico City) but in places
in those cities where at least one of us, and preferably both,
had never been. The purpose of this requirement was to
learn something from the place we had selected as well as
from the conversation of that day.

We talked, and looked, and pondered in museums dedicated to strange obsessions, in little known art spaces and
galleries, in libraries, in cemeteries, in lecture halls, or meet-
ing rooms where topics we thought might have a bearing on
what we set out to do were being discussed, and we even met
in a hospital emergency room in the largest medical center in
the world just to see what kinds of things were being said,
what kinds of things held back. We let the eclectic venues
guide and inspire us. It was outside the National Yiddish
Book Center in Amherst, for instance, that the topic of
silence, one that has occupied Stavans for decades, first
emerged. And that topic led us to freedom of speech, and
that to freedom of action and belief, a topic that Neal Sokol
began exploring in *Eight Conversations*, specifically focusing
on the influence Isaiah Berlin had on Stavans. That influence manifests itself in these playful pages.

The connection between the reflections and interviews is
deliberately understated. The former are impressionistic,
offering a sense of Stavans's rambunctious mindset. In contrast, in the latter I attempted to expand on them by pushing
him to explore a particular topic from myriad perspectives.
For instance, in "The Process Glitch" he mentions that in

the English language there are two words for the same concept: freedom and liberty. Are they one and the same? In the interview on dictionaries, he delved into the duality. And he returns to it in his discussion on the censorship and the writer, where he talks about John Stuart Mill and Nadine Gordimer, among others. Therein, in a nutshell, a map to his mind: expansive, centrifugal, dithyrambic.

When Ella Georgiades took a maternity leave, Luba Ostashevsky stepped in to steer the project to its completion. Both have been invaluable and we are indebted to them. And to Joanna Mericle, a blessing throughout the editorial process, a huge thank you. My gratitude goes to my indefatigable colleagues Martín F. Yriart and Eliezer Nowodworski for their counsel. Their knowledge is admirable, as free from any kind of censorship as is possible. I also appreciate the encouragement of the scores of readers who have sent insightful electronic messages in response to the work I've done with Stavans over the years. Finally, *gracias* to Neal Sokol for preparing the index. The material in this volume first appeared, in somewhat different form, in various periodicals, to whose generous editors, Gabe Bokor of the *Translation Journal*, and Robert Hartwell Fiske of *The Vocabula Review*, my gratitude is hereby acknowledged. (A note to curious readers: Three of the four dialogues included in *Knowledge and Censorship*—on "Dictionaries," on "Censorship," and on "Libraries" predate, but in may ways shaped, our conversations on love that led to *Love and Language*, a book on this most elusive of human emotions.)

—*Verónica Albin*

PART 1

Four Meditations

CHAPTER ONE

The Process Glitch

In an interview a teacher made with me some years ago, he asked, perceptively, if in identical settings a couple of students of different ethnic backgrounds would process the same information in different ways. The answer, of course, is a rotund no. None of us is a robot, responding mechanically to the stimulation that comes from the outside. Every individual reacts uniquely, spontaneously, even when coming from the same milieu. But then my interviewer narrowed down the field by suggesting that I imagine a set of boys whose adoptive parents are white: one of the kids is Latino, the other Asian. They receive the same feedback at home; at the request of their parents, they are placed in the exact same classroom through elementary, middle, and high school, and also enroll in the same college and pick the same major. Can we expect that one will see the world as a Latino and the other as an Asian? Or will the educational system erase genetic differences? It's a theoretical question, of course. None of us behaves as a robot exclusively defined by the DNA we have stored in ourselves. The opportunities that surround us shape our character and model our behavior. Still, as citizens of the United States in the twenty-first century, a country defined by an increasingly multiracial population, such a scenario isn't farfetched. In fact, I often come across "special" cases like the one my interviewer asked me to consider: raising children of different ethnicities under the same roof. In fact, with widespread international adoptions, it is now quite ordinary to see multiracial adoptive families. Putting aside for a moment the truism that every person is unique, is it likely to expect a response to knowledge from these boys defined by their Latino and Asian ancestry?

The answer I gave my interviewer was that knowledge is a process. What we know—information, skills—is a result of our interaction with others. What we know is what we learn and what we learn comes from a databank accumulated throughout the ages. But our DNA does shape our disposition. Cultures, defined as a set of beliefs shared by a people, have patterns: some emphasize memory whereas others endorse a more practical view of the world. A Frenchman and a German will be different not only because of their individual qualities but also according to the culture that shaped them. It's enough to open a number of dictionaries in different languages on a single word—say the word "honor"—to realize that each culture defines the emotion in singular terms. Although all men *aren't* created equal, the purpose of a democratic, pluralistic system is to grant everyone the same rights, regardless of their aptitudes and predispositions. The objective of education within that system is to offer all students a basis that allows them to recognize their strengths and grow.

The pursuit of knowledge was what drove me from my teens to adulthood. However, I've become a skeptic recently, wondering to what extent the knowledge I've accumulated has also made me blind. How do I know what I know? I'm not interested in the old philosophical idea of how can I know that I know, which to me is preposterous. Instead, what appeals to me is to trace the acquisition of knowledge that led me to be the person I am today. What made me become a teacher? When did I fall in love with books—or better, with the words they contain? At what point did I understand the way to handle my emotions, in private and in public? Was I ever aware of the extent to which the culture that surrounded me shaped my identity? How about my Polish—that is, Eastern European, Caucasian—ancestry? My being raised on *tacos, tamales, tcholent,* and *tzimmes?* In other words, when did I become the me that is me?

Consider politics. I was born and raised in Mexico, where politicians have always been seen as charlatans and the entire political apparatus as corrupt. The concept of a political leader able to selflessly escort the masses through rough times in fresh, innovative ways is taken by people with a grain of salt. When I moved to New York, one of the first culture shocks I went through had to do with politics. Back then there were far less jokes floating around about American politicians than there are now. I discovered that unlike in Spanish where we just have one word for politician, in English this creature was a two-headed beast: the politician and the *politico.* The concept of going to the voting booth on election day to choose a president, senators, congressmen, and governors was alien to me because in Mexico, even if elections were held, the final result was invariably decided beforehand behind closed doors. There, the selection of a successor to the president was traditionally entrusted to the incumbent president, and his finger (*el dedo*) invariably pointed to the one who was to be "democratically" elected (a process known as *"el dedazo"*). It's no surprise that my American reeducation—I came north when I was twenty-five—was about acquiescing as a civilian. In my native country I had been an activist, participating in political marches, getting involved with various community groups. That involvement aimed to bring true democracy to Mexico. In other words, it was a complaint against the bankrupt system we lived in. People would sometimes get beaten by the police; others would be imprisoned; still others, much less fortunate, would be shot or made to disappear without a trace. Clearly, manifesting one's views, while allowed on paper, was dangerous. We lived in a state of precarious freedom. Or should I say liberty? Why does English have a need for two terms? According to the *OED*, obsessed as it with etymology, "freedom" was coined in the twelfth century, whereas "liberty" was adopted from the French roughly two hundred years later.

In the United States, freedom is assured to everyone by the Constitution. There are regimes in other parts of the globe that are inclined to curtail that freedom. But the concept is ingrained in the culture to such an extent that the overall structure of American society depends on it. Individualism is the law of the land. The operative term is "tolerance." As long as I tolerate my neighbor, I'm entitled to be tolerated too. I might not love him or even respect him, but I must recognize his right to act freely; otherwise my own freedom is in question. What fascinates me about the American experiment is that—lo and behold—it works! Individuals from around the globe come in search of a better life. Once they're in, they begin a process of reeducation not unlike the one I went through myself. They adopt a set of values that includes everything: politics, yes, but also religion, health, music, fashion, cuisine. Just like in any culture, Americans have a unique way of dreaming. For an immigrant to make that way his own in a brief period of time is, in my view, miraculous.

Needless to say, there's a difference between ethnicity and culture. In the scenario my interviewer imagined, the boys are ethnically different, one Latino, the other Asian, but they share the culture of their American parents, teachers, and mentors instilled in them. Unlike the immigrant who came from elsewhere like me and was thus educated differently, the two will have gone through the process glitch, that is, the grinder (home, classroom, community center) through which we acquire the set of beliefs that makes us citizens of a single country. It is neither their present nor their future that is different, but their ancestry. That ancestry isn't fate but it surely defines character. An Irish American, an African American, a Polish American, a Chinese American, a Jewish American, and so on—we're all different, sure, but we all belong to the same club: the United States. It's a club whose survival depends on endorsing differences while stressing similarities.

There's another aspect of knowledge that intrigues me: its connection with language. Think of verb tenses: they allow us to have a sense of history. History is only possible in a civilization that uses a language capable of tense and aspect. To be able to talk about past, present, and future events allows for a teleological conception of time. This implies that our vision of reality is circumscribed by the limits of our language. Is it possible, for instance, that another dimension of time would exist if only our language would allow it? Scientists, obviously, will laugh at the assumption. Some of them support the view of language as an instrument to describe nature, and not as nature itself. Others, such as the early work in linguistics by Noam Chomsky, argue that grammar is embedded in our DNA before birth. But there is little doubt that different cultures see time differently depending on the syntactical structure they use. A novel by Austrian writer Peter Handke progresses at turtle speed, or at least that's the impression one gets, because for pages on end the verb keeps on evading the reader, waiting patiently at the end of the sentence. Yet if culture has an impact on language, ethnicity does not. Say the native language of the boys my interviewer invoked is English; hence, they'll express themselves in it, building their identity in the process. Their differences, however, become patent in attitudes, predispositions, desires. These aren't defined by language, at least not tangibly.

CHAPTER TWO

Wor(l)ds

I've been reading "island" novels. I call them that way because, after spending pleasurable evenings with them in remote scenarios with fanciful characters testing their stamina, I realize the narratives amount to a solid literary tradition: narratives set, in part or in full, in deserted islands. The adjective is essential. Manhattan is an island and so are Cuba and Australia. The stories I've been reading take place in uninhabited islands, some of which exist while some don't. Think of *Robinson Crusoe* by Daniel Defoe, *Utopia* by Thomas More, *Gulliver's Travels* by Jonathan Swift, *Lord of the Flies* by William Golding, *The Invention of Morel* by Adolfo Bioy Casares. The idea is clear-cut: to place a character in a distant, disconnected setting in order to appreciate the effects of civilization. Of course, there are other novels that without an island per se achieve a similar effect; *The Jungle Book* by Rudyard Kipling comes to mind. There are also the films—*The Enigma of Kaspar Hauser* by Werner Herzog and *L'enfant sauvage* by François Truffaut.

My interest, when it comes to these tales, lies mainly in language. How would an individual left to fend for himself in an uncivilized setting acquire a syntactically defined speech? In some of these imaginary plots the protagonist almost exclusively utters guttural sounds until a more consistent contact with people takes place. That is the norm: in a feral environment, a human living alone acts like an animal. That is, language, understood as an exchange of prearranged sounds linked to particular meanings, only exists when two or more humans interact. And then again that language develops into a sophisticated system once the humans discover the value of an exchange.

The same effect, by the way, is to be found in a person involved in an accident or struck by an illness, whose memory is suddenly erased. A stroke patient who suffers from aphasia, for instance, might have trouble remembering words or have a limited use of vocabulary. Because of aphasia and amnesia, certain words might have lost their meaning for him. And not only words but entire world-views might change. Last Sunday I read a column in the *New York Times Magazine* written by a woman who has been talking publicly about dementia. In a handful of paragraphs, she detailed the way her family was preparing to take a vacation when her husband of many years suddenly told her he wasn't going. He apologized while offering a trivial excuse. He convinced the woman to go on with the children without him. Once they were away, he sent a letter notifying her that he had filed for divorce. What followed was years in which the husband, taken over by mental illness, lost control of his emotions—and wrecked his life. The story wasn't delivered in any emotional way. The diagnosis, clearly, was a form of dementia that progressively affects one's life. At one point the husband would use caring, affectionate words with her and shortly after he would be irascible in previously unknown ways. He would use the exact same words to either love or injure his spouse.

To use words is to engage in abstractions. A clock and the word "clock" are two different things: one is an object, the other a preestablished set of sounds that refers to it within a certain context. The feral child in Truffaut's movie wouldn't know what the word clock meant until someone used it while pointing to a clock. In several of the tales I've been rereading, the contrast between what the narrator knows beforehand and the newly discovered island he encounters is shocking. Indeed, the pleasure of the narrative is to be found in the fact that there are elements on the island (objects, regions) utterly foreign to the visitor—and to the reader, too.

I've never lived on a deserted island. In fact, memory might be playing tricks on me but I might never have visited one. I'm no exception. When we travel, most of us visit recognizable settings where other people have lived for ages. Going to undiscovered landscapes is a dream but little more. Although I confess to often envisioning a sojourn to a distant land (a high mountain, a remote monastery, a secret cave), the truth is that what I like most is my comfort: the comfort of home that grants me proximity to my family, my books, my desk. Furthermore, how many deserted islands are there left today? The world has become a small place.

Still, the hypothetical experience is appealing because it points to the importance that language has in shaping our worldview. To live on an island is to be the master of one's domain. But is it possible? If we actually lived on one for a period of ten years, for instance, would our language change? How many words we wouldn't find usable would slowly fall out of our database? Would we come up with new words to describe objects, sites, possibilities we might discover on the island and whose existence isn't contemplated by the vocabulary we use? Furthermore, say we returned home after a decade, would we be shocked to hear words that came into existence while we were away?

All this makes me think about the words we use on a daily basis. It's impossible to estimate the maximum amount of words a person might remember at a given time. People of different economic strata, education, and age have their own lexical arsenal. Add to it the fact that each of us uses words in a rather loose way, depending on what we hear in our environment. That bank of words grows and it is put to use at an amazing speed in childhood. We know what milk is because we learn to associate it with the white pasteurized liquid that comes from a carton just like later we build on our definition of milk when we learn that it comes from cows, or, if born in the right place, goats, ewes, yaks, and camels. Each of those words is a world onto itself. When exposed to language, the child is exposed to a particular understanding of reality.

I used the word "arsenal." It has a military spirit to it. Maybe that spirit is fitting to the experience of interacting with others, which might be seen as a maneuver through which we make clear what we think. Choosing the right word isn't always easy but it's essential. For the way we articulate words is an expression of our intellectual freedom. What we say is as important as how we say it. The sentences we utter are our weltanschauung, a portrait of the universe as we perceive it.

CHAPTER THREE

Stealing Books

One day when I was about twenty years old, on an outing with my father in Ciudad de México, I was parking the car on the street. The back seat had a pile of books and little else. Just as I was about to lock the door, my father said: "Don't you worry, Ilan. No one steals books in this country." And he added: "In fact, the day they do we'll all be better off." I laughed at the idea but, as a challenge, deliberately left the door slightly open. We went about running errands and, when we returned, the car was intact. A month or so earlier I had left a leather jacket where the books were now. It took me less than ten minutes to stop by a drugstore and pick up antibiotics. I remember perfectly well locking the car. But the door was opened with the help of a wire hanger, a method the city thieves used at the time, and the jacket—nothing too fancy, by the way—was gone.

The day books are stolen in Mexico, we will all be better off. The statement stayed in my mind ever since. In fact, I've used it as a mantra. Several more times after that incident, I stored books in the back seat and left the car open. They were never touched. But on one occasion, a hilarious incident happened: when I returned to the car and inspected the pile, I realized there was one extra book, on a topic (algebra) I had no interest in whatsoever. Not only had my property been left alone; I had actually gained a volume.

The prohibition against theft is the Eighth Commandment (seventh for the Catholics and Lutherans). To take someone's possessions is to infringe on their right to property. Yet somehow the stealing of books appears to be on a category all its own. The amount of books I've lent over time far exceeds the amount I've gotten back; in other words, when it comes to sharing my books, I'm always at a deficit. And I'm also guilty myself, of course. Not too long ago, while making an inventory of my personal library, I discovered about a dozen titles, make that twice as many, that weren't originally mine. I had borrowed them from family and friends and somehow failed to return them.

Failed to return them? Did I ever have the intention of doing so? Sharing books, on the surface, is an act of generosity: if I like a novel I've read, I want others to experience the same aesthetic satisfaction. But for people like me, who have a personal library and, thus, collect books because there is a need to have them around, to see them as companions, as fellow travelers in the intellectual journey, the business of sharing is more problematic. And keeping what isn't ours? A personal library, like an ID card, is an expression of self. It showcases one's interests high and low. Not only the items to be found in it but its organization contain DNA. How do I organize my books?

I started acquiring books when I was an adolescent. I didn't like reading until late in my teens. But when the activity caught up with me, I was enthralled. I would read for hours on end: novels, stories, history, autobiography, philosophical treatises. (Poetry is an adult taste for me.) And the more I read, the more I wanted to keep books around me. Every peso I saved, I would invest in new acquisitions. Soon I hired a carpenter to add shelves to my room, which a few months later were already not enough. By the time I moved to New York, at the age of twenty-five, I had close to 4,000 volumes. What could I do with them? I selected a handful to bring along with me (I discuss the painstaking effort to select them in *On Borrowed Words*); the others I left on consignment with my parents, other relatives, and some friends. I told them that as soon as I got my own place and enough money, I would send back for them. Of course, I never did. Why bring 3,975 books, mostly paperbacks, when, by the time I turned thirty, I already had a collection almost half that size of mostly English-language titles that I had started buying in the United States?

Early in 2005, a close friend of mine died unexpectedly of an aortic aneurism. I was devastated and had poor concentration for weeks on end. My appetite and sleep were irregular. As a therapeutic exercise, I tried writing about him. But our relationship in the months before he died had been thorny and the difficulties were still too fresh. It was then that I decided to reorganize my personal library. Alison, my wife, had been pressuring me to do it for a long time. I had moved to the United States to become a writer. The process of settling down in a new country involved accumulating books. By now I had close to seven thousand and hadn't had any shelf space for a good while. I had literally piles over piles of books strewn everywhere. The size of the library had become dangerous because of the weight. Several wall beams were cracking. The staircase to my third-floor office was filed with so many volumes stacked on the steps that on several occasions, while coming down, I had tripped and almost killed myself. Often I wouldn't even be able to find a title and, in desperation, would buy an identical copy online. Clearly, it was time to say goodbye to as many as possible. Over a couple of months, I kept the essentials and boxed the rest. I contacted several antiquarian stores, and donated about four thousand to local libraries. Also, when the amount became manageable, I invited friends to help themselves. As they wandered around the selection I was ready to part with, I thought about the difference between stealing books and giving them away. I had given my friends permission to pillage my library—or the remains of it. They were not engaging in an act of robbery. Once or twice, I was embarrassed by the fact that one or more of them found books I had borrowed from someone but failed to return. The failure had been intentional. My mother had been working for a Jesuit university and had been let go after an altercation. I, too, had worked as a teacher at the same institution. As an employee, I had taken advantage of the library privileges. When the incident with my mother took place, I had with me a dozen or so books. Such was my anger at the university that I stopped working in the place. And I refused to return the library books I borrowed. I convinced myself it was revenge. I have forgotten which titles they were—with one exception: the two-volume set of Oswald Spengler's *The Decline of the West.*

Stealing books from a library is much worse that stealing them from a friend. The library is designed as a system whereby borrowing is a privilege. The library books are owned by the library itself. But the library only exists in order to make them available to others—at no cost. Most libraries I've used belong to a school or community center; in other words, I'm a user because I'm affiliated with the institution itself. And unless I'm late in returning a book, I don't pay a cent. Indeed, one of the beauties of the library as a concept is that it doesn't involve money: I don't buy the book, nor do I pay to rent it. Symbolically, the book belongs to the community as a whole. Thus, stealing one of them is taking away from the public good.

Obviously, the feeling of revenge I experienced wasn't an exception. How often, in our daily affairs, do we go through similar emotions targeted not toward another individual but toward society as a whole? In his memoir *My Last Breath*, Luis Buñuel, one of my idols, talks about dreaming of blowing up a church or a government building. The individual is defenseless against institutions. He agrees to live by the rules set by these institutions. However, every so often there is a rightful wrong that is committed. What to do in such cases? How to let the anger out? Stealing books from a library, it strikes me, is wrong. But it's a minuscule wrong compared to larger, more aggressive antiestablishment reactions, the most complex of which is an act of terrorism.

Who is it that said that ignorance is a form of oppression? Manufacturing books is an essential part of the democratic endeavor. In order for a civil society to function in fair and balanced ways, information needs to be disseminated evenly. Hence, a library might be seen as a market where ideas are placed in front of our eyes for us to ponder them, to endorse the ones we empathize with. A personal library, however, serves a different function: it is not an open space but a statement of affinities. The books contained in it are a map to the owner's mind.

Growing up in Mexico, I was struck by the limited currency that ideas had in intellectual circles. Even though books were encouraged in my household, the culture of using a library wasn't part of my middle class education. It wasn't because my parents had a moral reaction to libraries as institutions. It was just that the library as a site of encounter, social, intellectual, artistic, wasn't the norm in Ciudad de México. On the contrary, they were frequently underfunded, their title selection embarrassingly limited. Worse even, the idea of borrowing and returning books wasn't part of the culture. Whenever I would visit a library, I would find, yet again, that the collections were decimated by delinquent readers: books were stolen, pages were ripped and crossed out, and nasty comments appeared as marginalia. Indeed, I remember visiting once the Hemeroteca Nacional, the periodicals library housed at the UNAM, the largest university in the nation. I was hoping to launch a career as a columnist and wanted to do research on Lázaro Cárdenas, who was Mexico's president in the late 1930s. When I asked the reference librarian, she told me the collection of newspapers I was after had almost totally disappeared—only a few bound volumes remained. I was dismayed. Shortly thereafter, I visited the library's public restrooms and found that most didn't have toilet paper. In its stead were newspaper pages that were cut in squares. The ones I used were from 1936.

The cemetery and the library: are there more significant places in any town? One points to the past, the other to the future.

CHAPTER FOUR

Keeping My Mouth Shut

The freedom to speak—what does it mean? It surely cannot mean the capacity to say whatever we want. For although that capacity exists as a right, to think and say what we please when we please, in truth the right is only symbolic. There is much one cannot say because of social, psychological, intellectual, and religious pressure. I might disagree with my neighbor's views about morality, for instance; and it is okay to express those views in a civil, respectful fashion. But I can't express them in a harmful fashion, otherwise I'm guilty of incendiary speech. The freedom to speak is an essential component of open societies. I am able to determine my own behavior, to carry myself as I want, but only within the limits of what's acceptable. And what is acceptable varies from one age to the next and from one culture to another.

At a recent roundtable I participated in, I shared the podium with a despicable person whose name shall remain unmentioned. His ways of conducting himself in public were offensive. To advance his argument, he used questionable tactics and demeaning language. A portion of the audience sympathized with him, seeing in him an emblem of resistance—to society as a whole as well as to the accepted rules of decorum. Every time he would open his mouth, people would either applaud or scream.

I was quite uncomfortable. In fact, I didn't understand the purpose of the entire exchange. He accused me of all sorts of sins, including perverting our young. As the evening developed, my emotions went from impatience to anger onward to resignation. As I reached that last stop, I realized the best way to handle the fellow wasn't through words but through carefully constructed silences. In other words, I realized the most foolproof response he should get from me was not on his terms but on mine.

I thus decided to keep my mouth shut. Was I curtailing my freedom of speech? No, because silence is another form of speech—the absence of speech. Each of us is born with the inalienable right to say whatever one wishes. But that liberty is often misconstrued. Circumstances often dictate what one says and how one says it. It isn't that circumstance is a form of censorship but that a set of words, orchestrated in the appropriate way, has an impact, whereas in other settings it might not. If Isaiah Berlin, an intellectual I admire deeply (my second child is named after him), had enunciated his views on freedom to an Andean tribe instead of at Oxford, their influence would have been minimal.

Furthermore, had he expressed them in an unruly, offensive fashion in the academic setting he chose, their effect would also have changed, in particular given the message of tolerance he advocated.

Keeping one's mouth shut is a democratic privilege.

PART 2

Four Interviews

with
Verónica Albin

CHAPTER FIVE

Knowledge

Information is not knowledge.
—Albert Einstein

Verónica Albin: How would you define the word "idea"?

Ilan Stavans: The *OED* offers a beautifully evasive definition: "The conception of anything in its highest perfection or supreme development." Of course, the definition is inspired by Plato's philosophy, which establishes ideas from the Greek *idein* as a heavenly semblance, an attribute, an abstract configuration. Along these lines, the *OED* says that idea is "the conception of a standard or principle to be realized or aimed at." It might also refer to something original: it was Jane Doe's idea! But idea, to me, is a particle of thought in its most succinct form—a representation, a conception, a mental image.

VA: Where do ideas come from?

IS: It could be argued, I suppose, along Plato's line of thought, that ideas are divinely inspired and that, using the terminology of today, somewhere in heaven there's a databank of ideas from which each of us regularly downloads his share.

VA: Is there?

IS: For idealists, there surely is.

VA: Are you an idealist?

IS: I am, no doubt. This conception suggests that no idea is ever new and that not only every thought we have has already been thought by someone else but that no idea, no matter how daring it is, is ever original. But there's the Aristotelian approach to the topic: ideas, according to this position, are spontaneous, chaotic, and individualized. The ideas each of us has are the result of a confluence between talent, circumstance, and thought.

VA: Can there be ideas without language?

IS: Anthropologists have demonstrated that *Homo habilis*, appearing at the beginning of the Pleistocene period, some 1.8 million years ago, was not capable of language, but most certainly capable of ideas. The Kenyan paleoanthropologist Louis Leakey was instrumental in these findings. His son Richard Leakey also a paleoanthropologist, wrote about them in *The Making of Mankind*, published in 1981. This protohuman was able to create mental maps and plot strategies that allowed him to fashion tools and follow prey. Furthermore, ideas can be expressed through music, architecture, painting. They do not require language, just thought.

VA: That's the direction I want us to take, Ilan: the shaping of thought. What is thought?

IS: The organizing of ideas in an orderly, coherent fashion. That organization might be articulated or not.

VA: So what you are saying is that ideas can be expressed through language, music, painting, or architecture, but they don't have to be expressed at all.

IS: Each of us has his internal monologue: what the modernists called "stream of consciousness" and the new agers "inner voice." It's a never-ending flux of thought.

VA: Is it visual?

IS: No, it's a sequence of insights, most of which vanish into thin air. As I wake up, I make a mental map of the activities I have immediately before me: brushing my teeth, shaving, taking a shower, getting dressed, having breakfast... I don't use either words or images to articulate it.

VA: What do we use instead?

IS: Thought.

VA: So is there thought without ideas?

IS: Maybe it's what comes before ideas. In any case, I don't believe our vocabulary is elastic enough to describe the process. Seventeenth-century English did not serve Shakespeare at all. He had to invent a language if he wanted to reach the human soul. But he was not the only one who had to overcome inadequate language for their geniuses. Montaigne had to depart from Rabelais, Dante had to leave inchoate Italian behind, and Cervantes had to invent a new Spanish just like Lessing and Goethe had to do it for German. Surprising that of all these great men, it was only Cervantes who was a soldier in the literal sense.

VA: Do you revert to our native Spanish when you have this internal monologue?

IS: My internal monologue doesn't take place in words. If, for instance, I have to make a phone call, I don't see the six words "Call Harold about dinner on Sunday" passing through my mind. Instead, I have the nonverbal idea. In my case, this happens even when the monologue is work-related. When I've been in the midst of completing a story (for instance, "The Disappearance"), I generally run several miles in the morning, at which time I sort out the plot. But at no point do I see the words themselves; I see images in my mind, and I push these images to perform, for me alone, a theatrical movement. The characters might talk to one another. If I'm not pleased, I set them in another stage where they might engage in other behaviors: being liberated by their captors, talking to the media, writing a letter, etc.

VA: Before we explore the connection between language and thought, let me stay a little longer on words themselves. In particular, the dissemination of the printed word and Gutenberg. Have you ever been to the Grote Markt in Haarlem?

IS: I see where you're coming from. Yes, there's that monument to Laurens Janszoon, the sexton of Sint Bavokerk, who some, especially the Dutch, think was the inventor of movable type.

VA: The story goes that when he was near death, one of his assistants, by the name of Johann Fust, stole his presses and type and took them to Mainz and to Gutenberg.

IS: But there is also one Panfilo Castaldi born in the Veneto sometime in the late-fourteenth century, in a town called Feltre, if I'm not mistaken, where I remember seeing a statue claiming that he was the inventor of the movable type.

VA: Everyone wants to get on the bus of fame. Whether Castaldi did or didn't, and most probably not, he ought to still make it into the history books for he was running very successful printings of the classics, including Cicero, in pretty difficult times, and that's good enough for me. But I brought Gutenberg up because I want to talk about a physicist wunderkind Blaise Agüera y Arcas and a librarian Paul Needham, keeper of the Scheide Library at Princeton University and intellect extraordinaire, who jointly delivered a lecture on January 27, 2001, before a standing-room-only audience at the very staid Grolier Club in New York City. That lecture shook the history of knowledge.

IS: Agüera y Arcas and Needham got to work on the Calixtus Bull, also known as *Bulla turcorum*, issued, of course, by the then-pope Callistus III, a Spanish pope, by the way, and printed by Gutenberg in 1456. This Vatican letter was a fund-raising effort to go fight the Turks.

VA: Was this the only Gutenberg document that they analyzed?

IS: They also used two bibles printed in Gutenberg types that are at the Scheide at Princeton.

VA: Conclusions?

IS: As is often the case with legendary historical figures, like Columbus and Freud, Gutenberg gets credit for an effort that goes beyond him. Nothing surprising about this. In "Borges and I," Borges writes—in Andrew Hurley's rendition: "I willingly admit that [Borges] has written a number of sound pages, but those pages will not save *me*, perhaps because the good in them no longer belongs to any individual, not even to the other man, but rather to language itself, or to tradition." Likewise with human inventions: they belong to no one specifically but to tradition.

VA: Do you believe this about your work as well, about your own legacy?

IS: Without a hint of doubt. Once I've done something, it is no longer mine. It belongs to the ever-changing river that is civilization.

VA: And memory...?

IS: And memory, which is equally unstable.

VA: Let's go back to the connection between language and thought.

IS: By language, I assume you're talking about words, sentences, paragraphs, etc. That is, verbal communication.

VA: Yes.

IS: Thought and language are intricately related. But thought exists outside language.

VA: Does it? Elsewhere you've said that the limits of one's world are defined by the limits of the language used to conceptualize it.

IS: And that whatever cannot be said doesn't exist...I see no contradiction. The stream of consciousness allowing us to be alive, responsive to our environment, doesn't materialize in a syntactically organized sentence. It exists only inside us. Still, our language *is* our weltanschauung: the perimeter of what we think, who we are, where we go is limited by the world in which we exist. And that world is only possible through language.

VA: What do people mean when they say their thoughts are "broken"?

IS: That they aren't able to synchronize an idea and the language available to describe it. Ideas are born in all shapes and forms. Some are aborted along the way, others come out lucidly refined. In my mind, one should always strive for the perfect delivery: an idea poorly articulated has a limited chance of survival.

VA: Conversely, I assume there are bad ideas that are well-articulated.

IS: Absolutely. The ultimate purpose of education is to endow the student with the confidence to think coherent thoughts and to have access to the right linguistic tools in order to communicate them eloquently in front of others. Education is a universal right.

VA: Everyone is entitled to a sound education.

IS: To the opportunity to "speak one's mind." Ignorance is oppression. Today, the population of the world, made of billions of individuals, is divided between the haves and have-nots. I'm not referring to money and material wealth but to access to knowledge. In an age like ours in which information is power, not to have access to it is to be marginalized.

VA: Would you say that the lack of access to information marginalizes people more than the literacy barrier of yore? In other words, is the gap between those who can read and write and those who can't smaller than the gap between those with access to information—say the Internet—and those without?

IS: Unquestionably. A few days ago, I read, with some 150 high school students, Genesis 11, sections 1–9, about the Tower of Babel, where the Earth is defined as "of one language, and of one speech." Then, in the land called Shinar (probably Mesopotamia), people built a city, and within the city a tower. Sections 5–9 in the King James version read:

> And the Lord came down to see the city and the tower, which the children of men builded. And the Lord said, Behold, the people is one, and they have all one language; and this they begin to do: and now nothing will be restrained from them, which they have imagined to do.

Go to, let us go down, and there confound their language, that they may not understand one another's speech. So the Lord scattered them abroad from thence upon the face of all the earth: and they left off to build the city. Therefore is the name of it called Babel (confusion); because the Lord did there confound the language of all the earth: and from thence did the Lord scatter them abroad upon the face of all the earth.

Polyglotism, in this biblical passage, is thus perceived not as an asset but as a punishment. In using a single language, the argument is made, people become arrogant and presumptuous to the extent of being ready to challenge the Lord's authority. So speaking not one but many tongues is a curse. But is it really? In any case, even though monolinguals are a minority worldwide, they aren't excluded from the circles of power. Translation, among other tools, is a way in. Yet those circles close up when the control of information—knowing how to manipulate language, how to articulate thought—isn't available.

VA: Can I ask you to also define the word "right"?

IS: As you might imagine, the *OED* devotes several pages to the term "right." For the purposes of this discussion, it defines it as "a legal, equitable, or moral title or claim to the possession of property or authority, the enjoyment of privileges of immunities, etc." In other words, a right is an entitlement. Since the French Revolution, our approach to rights in Western Civilization proceeds by means of equality. Everybody is entitled to the same entitlements. This is in contrast with earlier times, far more hierarchical, where individual entitlements depended on nobility and tradition.

VA: The fundamental rights?

IS: Yes, the right to life, to associate according to one's wishes, to be happy, to procreate, to embrace whatever religious faith one chooses. Democracy, in order to sustain itself, depends on these rights—and the American model serves as torch. Everyone is created equal and, at least at the outset, has the same chances. Needless to say, this is a concept in the field of jurisprudence. People are born unequal according to their religious, ethnic, economic, and political qualities. Even in industrialized democracies like England, Germany, France, and the United States, there are first- and second-class citizens. Although on paper all of them are endowed with the same rights, in truth they are differentiated by their background, ethnicity, education, and means. And then, obviously, there's the question of talent.

VA: Do you mean talent as an individualized characteristic?

IS: Nature doesn't make us equal. We have sets of identical twins where each is talented in unique ways.

VA: What does the adjective "inalienable" suggest when appended to the concept of right?

IS: It is a term that comes from English Common Law. It announces that fundamental rights cannot be transferred or surrendered. No matter what a person does or says, if he's handicapped, if his parents were criminals, the same rights that apply to everybody apply to him as well.

Again, I return to the concept of democracy. It's a most fragile system of social organization because it is based on a tacit contract: all men are created equal. That is, at the core of democracy is the idea of tolerance. I might not like your religion and you might not like mine, but in order to live happily and in peace, the two of us need to tolerate each other. Needless to say, tolerance and acceptance, even love, are dramatically different. I don't need to accept you in the sense of embracing your opinions. Nor do I need to love you or what you represent. My only requirement—and yours too—is rather minimal: to tolerate one another. I like the idea that the same word, tolerance, we use to describe endurance to pain is also employed to refer, as the *OED* announces, to "the disposition to be patient, to with or indulgent to the opinions and practices of others."

VA: You use the *OED* as if it were the Bible. Or perhaps the *Magna Carta*.

IS: Its roots are similar. Isn't the dictionary a compendium of lore, organized alphabetically, whose authority permeates every aspect of society? Obviously, nobody is condemned to death using the *OED* as a code of law. But it certainly is a code of knowledge.

VA: You've called it "our portable memory, transferable from one generation to the next."

IS: Except that every generation builds on it.

VA: A delicate matter, because not all dictionaries grow.

IS: True: some don't grow for good reasons, some for bad. Merriam-Webster's contemporary editions, for example, always stay about the same in thickness. That can only mean that they take out as much as they put in. But we can forgive them that because, as a descriptive dictionary, its chief editor Frederick C. Mish is constantly striving to reflect current use.

VA: And for bad, I'm sure you're going to talk about the *Real Academia Española de la Lengua*?

IS: Their official dictionary grows alright, but not always in a healthy fashion. The politics of linguistic exclusion they engage in are such as to leave out the parlance of substantial speakers of so-called bastard jargons in the Spanish-speaking word, which, as you know, has approximately 475 million people. One might ask, no doubt: can a single lexicon include the verbal heterogeneity of that large a population?

VA: The "Declaration of Principles on Tolerance," issued by UNESCO, defines tolerance in different terms: as "an active attitude" and a "responsibility that upholds human rights, pluralism (including cultural pluralism), democracy and the rule of law."

IS: Pluralism is the capacity to live as an island in an archipelago of difference.

VA: The U.S. Constitution mentions "the right to liberty, property, and the pursuit of happiness." Are these rights properly ranked?

IS: Not in my view. I would reverse the last two: freedom of speech, of enjoyment, and of ownership. In my opinion, property is almost insignificant.

VA: Are you talking about material property?

IS: And intellectual, too. I have a house in Amherst and another one in Wellfleet, clothes, a bank account, an automobile. Do I care about them? Not much, to be honest. I wouldn't savor my freedom and happiness were it not for the financial stability these possessions grant me. And therein lies the clue: all fundamental rights are interrelated. It is counterproductive to be free in one realm but not in another.

VA: I want to return to the central tenant of our interview: knowledge.

IS: Let me pose a question, for once: if people are unaware of their fundamental rights, do those rights exist? The question is not unlike the parable of the tree that falls in the forest, making a loud noise: if no one hears it, was there sound? And did the tree fall if there were no eyes to see it? However, when it comes to the law, the premise is different. Every person must abide by the law, regardless of if we know about it.

VA: But if we don't know about it, how can we abide by it?

IS: Think of a policeman who stops you on the road for going at eighty miles per hour. Assume you were unaware that such speed limit existed in a particular section of the highway, are you exempt from the fine as a result? You aren't, of course. While it is doubtful that every citizen has a copy of the U.S. Constitution at home, let alone the endless amendments, the rules set in these apply to everyone.

This discussion makes me think of Franz Kafka's story "Before the Law." A man awaits entrance through a door but the guard stops him right before it. Every attempt the man makes to go through it is met by defeat. At the end of the story, the guard closes the door, but not before telling the man that the door was built for him to go through but now it's too late.

VA: In Kafka's story, the guard appears to know why the door exists. Yet he keeps the man from succeeding in his task.

IS: That's exactly my point: the law is often used as an impediment, not as an encouragement. In Mexico, where I was born, this is often the case: the Constitution is a document whose standing isn't upheld by society; it simply exists on paper, its laws at times used in detriment of progress.

VA: A grim view...

IS: A realistic view. The meaning of the law changes from one society to another.

VA: Let's explore ethnic difference as it applies to knowledge as well as jurisprudence. The United States is increasingly becoming a multiethnic society.

IS: A benign transformation, in my opinion.

VA: Do different groups process knowledge differently? At the beginning of this interview, you insinuated that language and thought go hand in hand. And in your essay "The Process Glitch," you use the paradigm of the ethnically different siblings to discuss the acquisition of knowledge. Do we all learn the same way?

IS: The Nazis used race as a qualifying theory to justify the murder of millions of people. The same has been done by other tyrannical regimes, left and right: from Stalin to Mao, from Cambodia to Iraq. Racial theories are unacceptable. It's essential to recognize that different ethnic groups represent diverse cultural traditions. Equal access to knowledge and the recognition of fundamental rights might be a sine qua non in Europe. In other parts of the world, however, people are unaware of them. A multicultural society, to be successful, needs to be sensitive to different backgrounds.

VA: Are you suggesting that the same requirements don't apply to everyone, that the child of an immigrant from El Salvador should be expected to perform differently from one whose parents come from Croatia?

IS: Not quite. My suggestion is that the expectations change as society itself undergoes transformation. I hear common complaints of students nowadays dropping out of school. Actually, the situation is rather desperate in the case of Latinos. They are entitled to the same rights as everyone else. But are these students not learning altogether? Do they have a different approach to knowledge? No. But their respective cultures are defined by unique forces and, thus, the expectations they set for themselves differ.

VA: Emma Lazarus, in her sonnet "The New Colossus," describes the United States as a safe haven for the dispossessed.

IS: The last five lines of her poem, engraved in a plaque at the pedestal of the Statue of Liberty, read:

> Give me your tired, your poor,
> your huddled masses yearning to breathe free,
> the wretched refuse of your teeming shore.
> Send these, the homeless, tempest-tost to me,
> I lift my lamp beside the golden door!

VA: America as utopia.

IS: There was a time when the country did embrace the tired, the poor, the huddled masses yearning to breathe free. In fact, the Statue of Liberty itself was, until World War II, a symbol of maternal welcome, greeting immigrants arriving mostly from the Old Continent. But the Statue of Liberty has lost its value. Most immigrants today come not from Europe but from the so-called Third World: Mexico, Central and South America, India, Pakistan, the Arab world, and Asia. They aren't received with open arms. Most of them arrive by foot, dangerously crossing the U.S.–Mexican border. They are met with skepticism, disdain, and xenophobia. Will they advance the way previous immigrants did? In general, I'm optimistic. But after 9/11, I've become a bit more pessimistic. No, the nation is no longer a utopia.

VA: Was it ever?

IS: The Statue of Liberty with its noble words by Lazarus was dedicated in 1886, barely twenty-one years after the Thirteenth Amendment of 1865, to the Constitution when the United States had a population of nearly four million enslaved men, women, and children. Clearly, forced relocation, whether from Africa to the Americas or from the Ukraine to Siberia, has never been utopian. But take William Penn's experiment in West New Jersey. His frame of Government was the springboard for the U.S. Constitution.

VA: Will the United States ever succeed in becoming a color-blind society?

IS: Never.

VA: Let's tackle the subject of silence, one that has occupied you for decades, as it pertains to knowledge. In particular, I would like us to talk about one man, Cardinal Bellarmine— Galileo's Javert—who was canonized in 1930.

IS: Interesting man, but he should have read his Augustine better. The dispute was about science itself and the role it should play, not about a particular finding such as whether the sun orbits the earth or the other way around. It all had to do with the City of God, which, if Galileo was right, could never again be viewed in the same way.

VA: So his science, Galileo argued, could not be silenced except by a better mathematician or a better mind, and not by the Church and most certainly not by the cardinal.

IS: The Church, in Galileo's view, had no authority to describe the physical world.

VA: So if the Church could no longer say what is and what is not...

IS: Bellarmine was a modest man who had much to be modest about. He should have read Augustine carefully. Both the saint and scientist were brighter intellects who understood that there are two worlds, two kinds of reality. Let the scientists be the authority in the City of Man and let the Church rule over the City of God.

VA: Next, I would like to focus on dreams.

IS: Ah, dreams and knowledge. Is it possible to distinguish between the two?

VA: I've heard you're writing a personal book on dreams.

IS: A kind of memoir similar to *Dictionary Days: A Defining Passion.*

VA: If, as you've argued in this interview, cultures access knowledge in different ways, it follows that they have different patterns of speech—regardless of the language they use.

IS: That is, precisely, the field of study that Alison, my wife, works on: she looks at how children are socialized into language across cultures. From my experience, it's clear that Latinos, African Americans, Asians, Native Americans, and other ethnicities approach the world in unique verbal terms. The syntactical patterns they use, the way they construct speech, reflects their weltanschauung. And if knowledge is processed through language, then each culture formulates it in its own terms.

VA: How does a specific culture shape its own idiosyncrasy?

IS: Patiently, through the passage of time, by responding to the stimulation of its environment, by making choices. It's the exact same process a person goes through in developing an identity.

VA: Does the Melting Pot erase that collective identity?

IS: To some extent. The offspring of an Italian immigrant no longer use the Sicilian dialect of their parents. Yet the way they use the English language distinguishes them from their Jewish, German, Russian, or French counterparts. By the time the grandchildren of immigrants marry out of the flock, into other ethnicities, those traits disappear. Not altogether, though. In addition, there are always new immigrants arriving in the United States. Hence, the shaping of a national language is invariably defined by the clash between a homogenizing drive and the heterogeneity of speech in the world itself. Unity and multiplicity.

VA: A question about freedom and identity inside the Melting Pot. In the introduction to your book *Spanglish: The Making of a New American Language*, called "*La jerga loca,*" there is a mention of an exercise in translation you made with students, in which one of the participants rendered the "Pledge of Allegiance" into Spanglish.

IS: On July 4, 2007, I heard on the radio in Texas a similar translation of the first two paragraphs of the Declaration of Independence. I scrambled to transcribe it.

VA: Do you still have it?

IS: It is softer, more *castiza* than the one I did on the first chapter of *Don Quixote*:

> Cuando en el curso de human eventos se hace necesario que una gente disolva las bandas políticas que han conectado a ellos con otros y asumir entre los poderes de la tierra, la estación separada e igual que las natural laws y God's nature los intituló, un respeto decente de opiniones de la humanidad requiere que ellos declaren las causas que los imperaron a la separación.
>
> Nosotros cargamos que estas verdades son self-evidentes, que todos los hombres son creados iguales, que ellos están endowdados por su Creador con algunos derechos inalienables, que entre ellos están la Vida, la Libertad y la pursecusión de la Felicidad. Que para asegurar estos derechos, los goviernos son instituidos por el hombre, derivando sus justos poderes para el consentido de los governados, que cuando cualquier forma de govierno se hace destructiva en estos finales, es el derecho de la gente de alterarlo o abolirlo, y instituir un nuevo govierno, layendo su fundación en esos principios y organización de sus poderes en esa forma, y que a ellos les sean más parecidos los efectos de su Seguridad y Felicidad.

VA: Historical documents such as these are national treasures. Every modern nation is built around them. The fact that they are drafted in the nation's official language is essential. In translating them into Spanglish, aren't you attacking the collective self?

IS: Latinos are an integral part of that collective self.

VA: Are you testing the limits of freedom?

IS: I'm simply savoring them.

VA: These historical documents are inalterable. They are also sacred, like the Bible.

IS: Are they?

VA: Would you do the same with the Qur'an?

IS: I don't belong to the tradition with it at its center, the way I am part of Judeo-Christian civilization. Knowledge, to be valuable, needs to be tested. Likewise with freedom. Herein, the prayer "Pater Noster," which, in a version I did for a Brazilian family, is called "Father Nuestro":

> Father Nuestro que'stás in el heaven,
> sanctificado sea your nombre;
> bring to us your reyno;
> may your voluntá sea in the tierra and el heaven.
> give us hoy our pan for each día,
> excusa our ofensas,
> 'cause we also perdonamos those that have
>   been ofendidos.
> Don't lid us to la tentación,
> enfríanos del evil. Let it sea. Amén.

And "Ave María":

> Ave María. God te salve, Mary, full of gracia.
> El Señor is contigo,
> blessed estás tú between todas las mujeres,
> and blessed es el fruto de your wom, Jesus.
> Holy Mary, madre of God,
> pray for nosotros, sineadores,
> now y en la hora of nuestra death. Let it sea. Amén.

VA: How are dreams instruments of knowledge?

IS: Samuel Taylor Coleridge said in 1803: "God forbid that my enemy should ever have the nights and the sleep that I have had, night after night... As I live and am a man, this is an unexaggerated tale—*my dreams become the substance of my life.*" In other words, a person without dreams is like a tree without water. Through these sequences, we're able to make sense of the chaos that surrounds us.

VA: Yet dreams are chaotic...

IS: Dreams have their own grammar, incomprehensible to the rational self. We don't process the world through sleep in the same way we do through rational thought. But we process it nonetheless.

VA: Do you dream every night?

IS: Perhaps I do, although, like most people, I only remember a handful of my dreams, which is alright since I'm not in the business of interpreting them. In fact, I find the interpretation of dreams as a scientific discipline utterly absurd.

VA: Why?

IS: To answer, let me quote Charles Lamb, who in *Witches and Other Night-Fears* said that "there is no law to judge of the lawless, or canon by which a dream may be criticized."

VA: So you disagree with the effort to make the grammar of dreams legible?

IS: Yes, we don't dream in order to understand what goes on when we are awake but the other way around.

VA: Non-Western cultures also engage in the interpretation of dreams.

IS: Of course, but for nonrational purposes. The Talmud states that a dream left uninterpreted is like a letter left unread. It also cautions about finding in dreams a rationale for a certain behavior. Some civilizations approached dreams as prophetic. Or else, as channels to communicate with nature and the divine. These strategies are present in us as well—in the Bible, for example. There is wisdom in dreams, although it isn't rational.

VA: Returning to an earlier point, you believe that cultures experience the dream world in unique ways, just as they approach language in their own terms.

IS: No doubt. Historically, we've been stuck, in Western Civilization, in the concepts offered to us by Sigmund Freud and psychoanalysis. Carl Gustav Jung pushed those concepts into the realm of myth, but that push didn't get us far either. It is time to see dreams in more relativistic ways. Is the nature of dreams the same across time? Are the dreams dreamt by Cicero, Dostoyevsky, Gérard de Nerval, Edgar Allan Poe, and Gabriel García Márquez interchangeable? The question, I believe, is crucial. Even those who answer affirmatively need to explain themselves. How is that different languages have developed yet our dreams are exactly the same regardless of time and space? I, for one, have the opposite view. It's true that dreams use images, not words, as a narrative tool, and images remain static from one period to another, from this culture to the next. But the cadence of narratives is different.

VA: Can you prove your point?

IS: I can't but that doesn't mean it's false. I look at it as an empirical question researchers are afraid to tackle. Why do developmental psychologists study the patterns of speech across cultures? Because they have data before them. What is needed is a new discipline about dreams. I envision a battalion of future researchers going out to collect data about dreams. What kinds of dreams do we have in childhood? How does an Argentine child build her dream narrative? And a Turkish boy? How about a Bengali? Are the dreams an Aztec had in 1522, before the arrival of Hernán Cortés, the same a Mongol had in 1265, just as Marco Polo was about to reach the Great Kahn in Khanbaliq, the Mongol capital?

VA: Dreams are also an escape.

IS: Or maybe life is. Your comment brings to mind Emily Dickinson's poem #531:

> We dream—it is good we are dreaming—
> It would hurt us—were we awake—
> But since it is playing—kill us,
> And we are playing—shriek—
>
> What harm? Men die—externally—
> It is a truth—of Blood—
> But we—are dying in Drama—
> And Drama—is never dead—
>
> Cautious—We jar each other—
> And either—open the eyes—

Lest the Phantasm—prove the Mistake—
And the livid Surprise

Cool us to Shafts of Granite—
With just an Age—and Name—
And perhaps a phrase in Egyptian—
It's prudenter—to dream—

VA: Knowledge, then, is not data.

IS: It isn't, obviously. Access to data brings power, but processing that data is where creativity kicks in. Through dreams we interpret information. The art of reasoning does the same: it establishes a thousand points of contact. The choice one makes in connecting those points is what makes each of us unique.

VA: Let's return to our discussion on thought.

IS: So much of it goes to the dump...

VA: What do you mean?

IS: What amount of it in a person's life survives? Fortunately, a minuscule part. Would you care to know what Borges was thinking on August 12, 1963, while having a bowl of Corn Flakes for breakfast? His reasoning is in his correspondence to friends like Maurice Abramowicz, his illustrious essays, stories, and poems. And, yes, in the array of fascinating interviews he left to posterity.

VA: Do you enjoy interviews?

IS: Tremendously. Some are heavily edited, of course. But in the most spontaneous ones the reader gets closer to Borges's stream of consciousness, his inner self, that almost anywhere else in his oeuvre. I must enjoy an interview in which the interviewer becomes an alter ego, a double. Such dialogues make me think I'm inside a box of resonances.

CHAPTER SIX

Dictionaries

Words are like dogs: they bite...
—Groucho Marx

Verónica Albin: What is language?

Ilan Stavans: The use of standardized symbols to communicate in a structured and consistent fashion.

VA: Standardized symbols?

IS: Sounds make words and words are symbols. By circumscribing the sounds PE-YO-TE to the small, soft, thornless, blue-and-green cactus found in Mexico and in the Southwestern United States, society attaches a name to the object. The name represents the object and stands in its stead. Objects have specific words attached. This specificity is crucial, for if the cactus changed every minute, language would defeat its own purpose. It would be shaped by chaos.

VA: A dictionary, then, is a catalogue of symbols...

IS: . . . pertaining to a specific group of people.

VA: Jean Cocteau once quipped that even the greatest masterpieces of literature are nothing but a dictionary out of order.

IS: Yes, the whole of *Catcher in the Rye* is in the *OED*, ready to be unscrambled. Similarly, one could argue that a dictionary is a narrative in a state of fragmentation. Or else, in discombobulated format.

VA: Lovely word, discombobulated. It is the kind of gem we call in Spanish a *pentavocálica*, for it has all five vowels. But going back to "dictionary," Thomas Aquinas warned us to "Beware the man of one book." Does this maxim apply to dictionaries?

IS: Lexicons are most dangerous artifacts: they surreptitiously get under our skin, influencing every thought we have, every aspect of culture we engage in. Yet, I'm in awe at the sheer courage they distill. Any attempt to catalogue an entire language is a quixotic effort.

VA: You called lexicons "artifacts."

IS: An "artifact" is an object crafted by humans, usually of cultural or historical interest. I like the familiarity the word has with "artifice," which denotes cleverness. Lexicons are also artifices in that they are cunning devices used to trick or deceive people. Dr. Johnson in his *Dictionary of the English Language* of 1755 calls attention to the Latin root for "dictionary," *dictionarium*, then states: "A book containing the words of any language in alphabetical order, with explanations of their meaning."

And he quotes from Brown's Vulgar Errours: "Some have delivered the polity of spirits, and left an account that they stand in awe of charms, spells, and conjunctions; that they are afraid of letters and characters, notes and dates, which, set together, do signify nothing; and not only in the dictionary of man, but in the subtler vocabulary of Satan."

VA: One of my favorite etymologies is that of "intel lect." According to the *Arcade Dictionary of Word Origins*, it is derived from the Latin root *intelligere:* "to perceive, to choose between." This is a compound verb formed by the prefix *inter-* "between" and *legere:* "gather, choose, read." Thus, intellect means being able to read between the lines. Do you have a favorite etymology?

IS: The word "persona," which in Latin means mask. It was also used to describe the character played on stage by an actor. Over time persona has come to be understood as the part of one's character in display for others. This was used in contrast with "anima," a reference to the soul. (In Spanish there is also the noun *duende*, used, among others, by Federico García Lorca.) Thus, "personable" means sociable, possessing a pleasant demeanor. And the endless variations: personal, personality, personate, personhood. In Anglo-Saxon, there are the synonyms "people" and "persons." In Romance languages, a persona—a gorgeous word, by the way—is an individual.

VA: The etymologist finds the deadest word to have been once a brilliant picture. In Emerson's words, "Language is fossil poetry." Oliver Wendell Holmes conveyed a

similar idea when he defined "word" as the skin of a
living thought and said that whenever he felt like reading poetry, he would read his dictionary. How would
you define word?

IS: Words are the fabric we use to dress our thoughts.

VA: You suggest in your book *Dictionary Days* that each
culture has the dictionaries it deserves, which echoes
Gandhi's opinion that every man at fifty wears the face
that he deserves. You added that dictionaries are like mir-
rors, and, as such, are a reflection of the people that produced and consumed them. Yet Jonathon Green in *Chasing
the Sun* argued that of the two most influential lexicographers in the United States and England, Noah Webster
and Dr. Johnson, respectively, the former gives his readers
a low church, Republican view of the world whereas the
latter gives his readers an Anglican, Tory worldview. Green
further claims that what both men were doing, although
neither articulated it as such, was playing God—or, if not
God, at least Moses descending from the Sinai with the
Tablets of the Law. If dictionaries are indeed written by
a theocracy, if they are canonical and have authority, do
they truly reflect the wants of the consumer, as you claim
they do?

IS: Playing God is a common attitude...Every artist
and intellectual, regardless of talent, engages in it. The
ultimate yet impossible dream of the human mind is to
explain and codify the universe. The result must be legible to others. This means the piece produced has to please
others—in mercantile terms, it needs to be "consumed."

No lexicographer lives on an island: the data collected comes from the people and it goes back to them.

VA: Mark Twain quipped that in German a young lady has no sex, while a turnip has. In French, "vagina" is masculine; in Italian, "flower" is masculine. Germany is a fatherland while Russia is a motherland. Furthermore, in Spanish we have issues of size and worth happening conceptually when we juxtapose certain nouns with gender desinences like *barco/barca* and *charco/charca*. Of the languages you speak, which is the most idiosyncratic and why?

IS: Each language has its own idiosyncrasy. This is because languages are shaped out of spontaneous historical changes, not in a laboratory. The reason why Esperanto, the nineteenth-century "rational" language created by the linguist L.L. Zamenhof of Warsaw, Poland (part of Russia when he was active), and known today as "the language for the global village" (doesn't English now fulfill that role?), is so predictable is that it is genetically engineered, so to speak. With its twenty-eight letters, it has little by way of surprise. Personally, I love gender desinences in Romance languages: *el sexo* is masculine but *la sexualidad* is feminine. This is telling, isn't it?

VA: When you come across a newly published dictionary in a store, or one in somebody's shelves, what crosses your mind?

IS: First, I must say I marvel at its sheer existence. I ask: Is this yet another attempt at cataloguing human language?

How is this item different from any other? Might it be closer to perfection? Second, I browse through its pages, caressing them, jumping from one definition to another. My mind sets on a somewhat exotic target: what about the word "percolate"? Or else, "numismatic"? Third, I choose a mundane, consuetudinary word: "water," "fire," "air"... As you know, I have a passion for collecting lexicons. The collection is constantly expanding. In fact, these items have ended up pushing regular books out of the shelf. So, if I like what I find in the dictionary, there is a fourth step: I wonder if I can part ways from this appealing item. I generally end up poorer after these types of exposure. In time, though, after I study the dictionary in detail, I come to terms with its shortcomings. For the term perfection, although defined in them, doesn't apply to their achievement.

VA: Indeed, Henri Meschonnic argues that:

> "[Les] Dictionnaires [...] sont donc à merveille les lieux où lire entre lignes, où reconnaître, plus facilement qu'ailleurs, les conflits, les masquages des conflits, les clichés qui font l'album de famille d'une culture."
>
> Dictionaries, [...] are the best examples of texts that one should read between the lines, where the conflicts, the hidden and ignored oppositions, the clichés that make up the family album of a culture can be detected more easily than anywhere else.

For a general dictionary to be successful commercially, do you think it must reflect the ideological values of the public that is supposed to buy it—not what is practiced, but what is seen as an ideal, a Norman Rockwell tableau of words, so to speak?

IS: Even if it attempted not to reflect that weltanschauung, it would inevitably do it. We're all prisoners of our own time and place.

VA: In the early nineteenth century, Constantin François de Chasseboeuf, Comte de Volney, said that the first book of a nation is a dictionary of its language, but clearly he was not speaking about the chronology of events, as his statement is not borne out by facts he knew: the United States did not have its own dictionary—Webster's—until 1806, thirty years after it declared its independence from England in 1776. What, then, do you think de Volney meant?

IS: Much like *Beowulf* for the Saxons, the *Kalevala* for the Finns, the *Nibelungenlied* for the Germans, and the Icelandic sagas, the dictionary serves the function of a foundational saga, although not about a mythical hero in his quest for order, but about a language in search of collective definition.

VA: In all general lexicons, there are endogenous definitions that issue from the weltanschauung of the dictionary compilers about themselves, and exogenous definitions written by the compilers about those outside their own culture. Henri Béjoint said that "dictionary" is a term with a wide extension and a complex intention. In your travels through dictionaries, what have you found about identity?

IS: Lexicons aren't only reductivistic, they are also outright xenophobic. Still, they serve a purpose: to define a people's universe.

VA: Let's tackle the thorny issue of prescriptivism versus descriptivism in dictionaries.

IS: There are, as you know, two types of lexicographic approaches: the descriptive and the prescriptive. In the former the dictionary is but a record of the ways of speech available in a certain time and space. In the latter the dictionary has a normative approach: it doesn't only offer users a bank of available voices but it announces what is correct and what isn't. In my rebellious spirit, I tend to admire the absurd authority projected in prescriptive lexicons. Their dream is to normalize a language, to make it proper. This, needless to say, is utopian. Having said that, I must stress the dialectical nature between prescriptive and descriptive dictionaries. One cannot exist without the other. Language without limits descends to chaos: grammar, syntax, spelling…these are all prescriptive activities. But when the limits are set in stone without any room to be innovative, language becomes stagnant. For languages to survive, they need to be in a state of constant mutation. They need to engage in a give-and-take, to borrow and improvise new terms, and offer terms to other languages. In my eyes this type of promiscuous relationship is fundamental to keeping a healthy metabolism. They cannot take too much, otherwise their essence vanishes. Nor can they give too much because they would disintegrate the languages that surround them. This process is intimately connected to movements like imperialism, globalization, and colonialism. Imperial tongues like Greek, Latin, Dutch, French, Spanish, and Portuguese conquered by erasing—or at least eclipsing—regional ways of communication. Nowadays imperialism might appear to be more subtle, though not less effective. English is not only the *lingua franca* of the present, it is also an imperial tongue. But it is a mistake to believe that it only lends words and doesn't borrow anything. In fact, English is constantly absorbing foreign terms. Actually, its survival for over a thousand years is the result of its admirable elasticity.

VA: You close *Dictionary Days* with a definition from Gustave Flaubert's *Dictionnaire des idées reçues* of 1881— "*Dictionary*: Say of it: It's only for ignoramuses!" Flaubert's dictionary has been labeled by Green as "a masterpiece of deflation" that picks away at the safe banalities of the nineteenth-century French bourgeoisie. And there is, of course, Ambrose Bierce's cynical *Devil's Dictionary* of 1906. We might also add to this list Cheris Kramarae's and Paula Treichler's *A Feminist Dictionary* that defines "ability" as "ability is sexless." What do you make of word lists assuming dictionary forms?

IS: There is an essential difference between a lexicon and a word list. The first attempts to be comprehensive, covering every single aspect in a particular field, for example, a dictionary of applied mechanics, a dictionary of fashion, a dictionary of Dostoyevsky's oeuvre, etc. Word lists are less ambitious, more arbitrary. Indeed, they are individual attempts to map out a person's temperamental inclinations. What I enjoy about these moody volumes is their unconcealed subjectivity. Standard dictionaries come to us surrounded with a clout of authority. Word lists don't presume to have any authority. Of course, the fact that the likes of Flaubert and Bierce produced them does give them muscle.

VA: What do you think of Adolfo Bioy Casares's *Breve diccionario del argentino exquisito*? By the way, it doesn't include the term *mejicanada*, which Argentines use to describe an excess of Mexicanness in an act or figure of speech.

IS: Every culture has authors who, tired of creating Works of imagination, sit down to decipher their own lexicon. In Spanish, I love Bioy Casares's dictionary and also like Camilo José Cela's on cant, the language of crime and prostitution.

VA: To Anatole France, the dictionary was the universe in alphabetical order. In defining it, Dr. Johnson preferred an analogy based on Alexander Pope's *An Essay on Criticism*: "Dictionaries are like watches, the worst is better than none," even if "the best cannot be expected to go quite true." This interests me enormously, for I always start my translation classes with this question to my students: What is a dictionary? Of course, I get the expected answers from smart alecks: museums of words I have to carry in my backpack to come to your class.

IS: One needs to reach a certain age to fall in love with dictionaries. While one is young, one approaches language uncritically, as a tool. It is only after one realizes that words are not only malleable but transient—just like us all—that our relationship with these artifacts becomes more complex. I'm able to trace, with frightening precision, the moment this change occurred in me. In Mexico I had access to different languages (Hebrew, Spanish,

Yiddish, French, English...), but I didn't pay too much attention to their differences. *Silla, kisé,* chair—the fact that a single object could be described in various ways didn't much concern me. Somehow language and identity were not conflictive categories for me. It was not until after I immigrated to the United States, in the mid-1980s, that I realized that language defines us in an encompassing way. Dictionaries, of course, are more than museums of words; they are fashion stores, too.

VA: How are dictionaries fashion stores?

IS: They contain relics but also neologisms. Plus, in a Nietzschean cycle of eternal return, users rediscover terms and infuse them with new meaning. This is done by the so-called retro people. I have in my personal library the first two volumes (A–G and H–O) of J.E. Lighter's *Random House Historical Dictionary of American Slang,* a veritable lexicographic treasure trove. Look at how words like "hot" and "mad" have changed meanings over the last 150 years.

VA: There is a quote attributed to Emperor Charles V that reads: "With ambassadors I speak in French, with the ladies in Italian, with my horse in German, and with God in Spanish." As you state it in *On Borrowed Words: A Memoir of Language,* you speak four languages, are they all equally useful for expressing your fears, your desires, your innermost thoughts?

IS: Not at all. English is best for essays and lectures, Spanish for writing fiction and expressing emotion, Yiddish is unparalleled when it comes to offensive words, and Hebrew is perfect for etymological disquisitions.

VA: When you say that Spanish is best for fiction and emotion...

IS: I find Cervantes's tongue incredibly elastic and suitable to engage in daydreaming.

VA: This makes me think of the extent to which lexicons are misogynistic. The Feminist Movement coined the term *dicktionary* arguing that whatever their intentions, dictionaries have functioned as linguistic legislators that perpetuate the stereotypes and prejudices of their male writers and editors, systematically rendering women invisible in their pages. This produced a number of dictionaries, such as the aforementioned *A Feminist Dictionary,* which had a firm revisionist agenda. Then we also have works like *The Dictionary of Cautionary Words and Phrases* compiled by a gaggle of journalists from a range of major American cities that warns against using words such as "community," for it implies a monolithic culture, or "articulate," for it can be considered offensive when referring to a minority. As Tom Lehrer put it: "In my days there were words you couldn't say in front of a girl; now you can't say *girl.*" Should a lexicographer be allowed to rewrite century-old history from contemporary viewpoints?

IS: It would be fascinating to study, in chronological fashion, the way the word "woman" has been defined by lexicographers from the fifteenth century to the present. My favorite definition, nevertheless, is in Spanish and comes from Sebastián de Covarrubias, whose *Tesoro* appeared in 1611 and was published under the aegis of the Holy Office of the Inquisition. The first Spanish dictionary, however, was the *Universal vocabulario en latín y en romance*, published in 1490 by Alonso de Palencia. Next came Nebrija's *Lexicon hoc est dictionarium ex sermone latino in hispaniensem* and the following year he published *Dictionarium latinum-hispanum*. Even though in 1505 the Franciscan monk Pedro de Alcalá, making use of Nebrija's work, published his *Vocabulario arábigo en letra castellana*, the father of Spanish lexicography is considered to be Sebastián de Covarrubias. His *Tesoro de la lengua castellana o española* was used by the Real Academia Española as the prime source for the compilation of the *Diccionario de Autoridades*, which in turn became the *Diccionario de la lengua española*. In any case, Covarrubias writes about the word *mujer*: "Muchas cosas se pudieran decir de esta palabra; pero otros las dicen, y con más libertad de lo que sería razón." (Many things can be said of this word; but others say them, and with more freedom than reason allows.) Covarrubias then offers a long quote describing women for their lasciviousness. This is the only time in over one thousand pages where the lexicographer refuses to define a word. Could it be because he is afraid to express his own wantonness?

VA: I came across the name Hester Lynch Piozzi, more widely known as Hester Lynch Thrale, Samuel Johnson's friend. I know that Johnson is a hero of yours, as is made clear in the chapter included in *Dictionary Days* in which he pays a posthumous visit to your home in Amherst.

IS: Johnson had a breakdown at the age of fifty-six. He was rescued by the Thrales, the distinguished Henry and his wife Hester Lynch Salisbury. Hester Lynch Piozzi (her second husband's name) wrote a couple of books on her famous friend, *Anecdotes of the Late Samuel Johnson*, which came out in 1786, and *Letters to and from the Late Samuel Johnson*, in 1788. She was a hostess that rescued Johnson and had a literary salon frequented by the likes of Edmund Burke, David Garrick, and Sir Joshua Reynolds. But she was more than a hostess; she was a lexicographer—although this aspect of her career generated much criticism. She authored an etymological study called *British Synonymy* in 1794 and a two-volume history of words known as *Retrospection*, published in 1801. Some critics have disregarded her oeuvre as imitative of Johnson's, no doubt an offensive, nearsighted approach. In the annals of English lexicography, Piozzi holds a secure place, especially as a female role model. She met James Boswell in 1768 and had a famously competitive relationship with him, among other things because both tried to capitalize on Johnson's fame as biographers, although Boswell took much too long to complete his own assessment of his mentor.

VA: The total number of words found in Shakespeare's collected works and sonnets is fifteen thousand, and some of these are *hapax legomena*—words used only once in the history of the printed word—such as *honorificabilitudinitatibus*, which appears in *Love's Labour's Lost*, act V, scene I. Linguistic studies have shown that the average American high school graduate has a vocabulary of sixty thousand words. Steven Pinker has dubbed it a *tetrabardian* vocabulary. What do you make of this discrepancy?

IS: I'm surprised by the size: sixty thousand? I read somewhere that the average American uses only two thousand different words a day. Who is to know? These quantitative studies are nothing if not intellectual pleasers, designed to prove whatever theory the researchers have set out to explain. Does a person today in Stratford-upon-Avon, England, use a smaller or larger vocabulary than his counterpart in the same place at the time of Shakespeare's death in 1616? The answer, I suspect, is more. There are, after all, more words in the English language in the twenty-first century than at any previous time. This has nothing to do with wisdom. There is simply much more to know nowadays and more accumulated ways to express it.

VA: Alison, your wife, is a speech pathologist and you are a writer. It is an interesting merging of views on language sleeping in the same bed, and this must have an influence on your children, Josh and Isaiah. In the first chapter of *Dictionary Days*, Isaiah asks you whether words die.

IS: At home we make endless jokes on and around language. You say potato and I say potahto...My kids are always correcting my English. Or else, they make fun of my accent and explain to me idioms I'm unfamiliar with as a nonnative speaker. Isaiah's question about the death of words intrigues me deeply. He wanted to know if there is a heaven where words might go. I told him there was: the dictionary.

VA: You and Alison chose to name your second-born son in honor of Isaiah Berlin. Berlin, a political philosopher and the author of *Two Concepts of Liberty*, had Russian as his mother tongue and English as his adopted academic language. Both of these languages make a semantic distinction between "freedom" and "liberty." One of Berlin's maxims is "Liberty for wolves is death to the lambs." Why did Berlin choose "liberty" over "freedom"?

IS: According to the *OED*, "freedom" is the power or right to act, speak, and think as one wishes without hindrance or restraint. It is the concern of the individual. "Liberty," on the other hand, approaches the same concept but from the societal view. It is a concept that affects people from the outside and structures their freedom. It is the state of being free within society from oppressive restrictions imposed by authority on one's way of life, behavior, and political views. Wolves and lambs are free to act as they wish. As animals they are motivated by sheer instinct, but as humans we live within moral confines. Liberty for Christians should not be death to other religious groups. Isaiah Berlin explored the concept of negative freedom, for example, not offensive, destructive freedom, but freedom within certain parameters. One might ask: is restricted freedom still freedom? The answer is an unquestionable "yes": there is no such thing as unrestricted freedom. Freedom invariably takes place within what is possible.

And in society what is possible and what is necessary need to go hand in hand.

VA: Anne Fadiman has said that Americans admire success while the British admire heroic failure. I quote:

> Who but an Englishman, Lieutenant William Edward Parry, would have decided, on reaching western Greenland, to wave a flag painted with an olive branch in order to ensure a peaceful first encounter with the polar Eskimos, who not only had they never seen an olive branch but had never seen a tree? Who but an Englishman, the legendary Sir John Franklin, could have managed to die of starvation and scurvy along with 129 of his men in a region of the Canadian Arctic whose game had supported an Eskimo colony for centuries? When the corpses of some of Franklin's officers and crew were later discovered, miles from their ships, the men were found to have left behind their guns but to have lugged such essentials as monogrammed silver cutlery, a backgammon board, a cigar case, a clothes brush, a tin of button polish, and a copy of *The Vicar of Wakefield* These men may have been incompetent bunglers, but, by God, they were gentlemen.

What cultural traits do you see in the pages of the *OED*?

IS: Was it George Bernard Shaw who said that England and the United States are two countries separated by the same language? Language is only a conduit to express oneself. Culture is a much larger category. In the Mexico of my adolescence one often heard jokes about Argentines, who are supposed to have huge egos. These jokes were often cruel: How does an Argentine commit suicide? He climbs up his ego and jumps. Why are Argentines buried in caskets with holes in them? Worms can't stand them either. By the way, there was a plethora of jokes about Mexicans in Argentina. Why don't Argentines eat Mexican refried beans? They know how to cook them right the first time around. Between these two nations there was—and still is—much misunderstanding, as well as envy.

VA: The *OED* has been described as a dictionary for decoding literary texts. According to the Dictionary Society of North America, the writer it quotes the most is Shakespeare (32,886 quotes), then come Scott (15,499), Milton (11,967), and Chaucer (11,000). The bias toward literature is so strong that the *OED* contains literary *hapaxes*, and words of marginal importance used by these preferred writers are rarely omitted and are usually assigned main lemma status.

IS: From Dr. Johnson to the present, the British are a stuffy people. The goal of the *OED* was to legitimize the English language by calling attention to England's stellar literary tradition. As we move from words to graphic signs in our civilization—middle-class children today are raised on a hefty diet of DVDs—literary quotations appear useless. It is not improbable that in the not-so-distant future the *OED* will come out with a lexicon legitimized by movie references.

VA: The strongest criticisms leveled against Murray's *OED*, released in 1928, were that its coverage of words native to North America was notably deficient, that words considered vulgar or taboo were not admitted, and that the vocabularies of science and technology, commerce and industry, were largely ignored.

IS: It is no secret that dictionaries are exclusive, not inclusive. No matter how hard one tries, one cannot avoid this shortcoming. After all, we're all prisoners of our own time and place. Plus, there is no denying in that each and every one of us approaches the world with a bias. Take James Murray, whose full name was James Augustus Henry Murray. He, whose patience, wisdom, and dedication made the first complete edition of the *OED* possible, was a Borgesean character. Simon Winchester succinctly described his lifelong effort as wanting to tackle "the meaning of everything." His unrelenting appeal to readers for citations, the Spartan rigors of his Mill Hill Scriptorium, the overall fastidiousness with which he approached his endeavor are all admirable and without peer. But Murray still felt marginalized from academia, for the Oxford dons did not treat him as an equal. This, in part, was what made him decide to exclude commercial and technical terms from the fascicles he progressively produced. In his eyes, gentlemen did not talk about money, machines, or business; gentlemen engaged in discourse about literature and ideas. Of course, contemporary bias in dictionary-making may be the result of an entity such as the Soviet Bureau, or, for that matter, of a monarch—such as Queen Victoria. The first edition of the *Concise Oxford English Dictionary*, from 1911, is full of subjective definitions, and so is the *Chambers Twentieth Century Dictionary* up to its most recent edition, the ninth, in 2003. Such subjectivity, which John Algeo called the "Johnsonian effect," may now be more restrained, but is certainly not absent from modern dictionaries. Yet, one could argue that those biases are no longer the result of individual idiosyncrasy, as they were in the times of Johnson, Emile Littré, Pierre Larousse, and Noah Webster. Now the slants, the prejudices, are those of a team of compilers—an Academy.

VA: In the essay "Of Jews and Canons" (*The Essential Ilan Stavans*), you mention that after reading Harold Bloom's book *The Western Canon* you came across a review in amazon.com from a reader in Spain who said that Bloom's book was not a Western canon at all, but "an English language one." You say that in Dr. Johnson's times, which you have branded a "less skeptical age than ours," Truth, with a capital "T," was "undeniable and absolute." Based on these observations, is the *OED* part of the Western canon?

IS: Without a doubt the *OED* is an integral part of the Western canon. It is a masterpiece of epic proportions, and its views of the universe permeate everything.

VA: Universe?

IS: Nothing is alien to it. Ludwig Wittgenstein in his *Tractatus Logico-Philosophicus* of 1921 said: "What can be said at all can be said clearly." Seven years later, James Murray proved Wittgenstein right.

VA: I came across in *A Guide to the Oxford English Dictionary*, composed by Donna Lee Berg, a reference to a certain Marghanita Laski (1915–1988), a British writer and journalist who often wrote under the pseudonym of Sarah Russell.

IS: There are other female contributors too, among them Ms. E.F. Burton of Carlisle, who contributed 18,700 citations, and the sisters Edith and E. Perronet Thompson of Bath, who contributed 15,000 and are frequently acknowledged for their proofreading efforts as well. And two of Murray's daughters, Rosfrith and Elsie, were important contributors, as was a daughter of editor Henry Bradley, whose name I have not been able to find and has perhaps been lost to history.

VA: What about Marghanita Laski?

IS: Although a professed atheist, she was a Marxist Jew from Manchester and the niece of Harold Joseph Laski, an Oxford alum who led the Labour Party between 1945 and 1946. Harold Laski taught political science at Yale and Harvard. Marghanita Laski has been the subject of some scholarship of late. She is the author of the book *Ecstasy: A Study of Some Secular and Religious Experiences*, which, to some, is of the caliber of William James's *Varieties of Religious Experience*. In the annals of lexicography, with her quarter of a million citations submitted—and all accepted, by the way—to the *Supplement* and the second edition of the *OED*, she stands as the supreme contributor, male or female, to the *OED* and is yet to receive the credit she deserves.

VA: In America, the tradition of "encyclopedicity" goes back at least as far as Noah Webster's *A Compendious Dictionary of the English Language* (1806), which had, among other things, tables of foreign currencies, ancient and modern weights and measures, a history of the world, Jewish, Greek, and Roman calendars, and a complete list of all the post offices in the United States. However, R. Bailey mentions an abridged edition of Dr. Johnson's *Dictionary* published not long after his death that includes weights and measures, a table of heathen deities, Archbishop Ussher's history of the world with principal dates from the creation in 4004 BC, and the market days in the principal towns of England and Wales.

IS: Johnson was always conscious of his stature. He understood his role as pathfinder.

VA: Yes, but would he have objected to these appendices or, more to the point, to the nature of these particular appendices?

IS: He would have, for sure. Johnson loved straightforward language. The circumvolutions, academicisms, and metaliterary devices we're accustomed to would have driven him out of his mind.

VA: You have a meditation on him in *Dictionary Days* in which you imagine Johnson visiting you at your Amherst home to discuss lexicography.

IS: Have you ever been asked: "If you had to choose a luminary from the past to have a conversation with, who would it be?" Samuel Johnson is one of the most verbally sensitive, intellectually lucid minds ever to walk this earth. I cherish his words like jewels. I have a solid collection of his oeuvre in my personal library. It sits next to my *Don Quixotes* and to my multiple Borgeses.

VA: In 1893 the U.S. Supreme Court used the dictionary to define "tomato" either as a fruit or vegetable in order to determine whether importing tomatoes was subject to tariff. It is worth noting that the word "dictionary" is often used in the singular, and with the definite article, as if there was only one dictionary per language, which would come in different formats and different types of presentation, but would contain the same information. But what is extraordinary is that in most court cases where dictionaries have been used as evidence, neither the title nor the exact nature of the dictionary used were disclosed. This has prompted Rosamund Moon to call this fictitious legal dictionary the UAD, *The Unidentified Authorizing Dictionary*, a mythical object everyone uses yet no one ever sees. You have coined the term *logotheism*. Similarly, in 1989 historical linguist John Algeo coined the term *lexico-graphicolatry*. How do these terms differ? And, if there is a logotheism, are dictionaries Scripture?

IS: *Logotheism* is a religious manifestation where words have center stage. Judaism and Christianity are logotheistic. Just think back on the first line of Mathew: "In the beginning was the word." The original term is *logos*. Also, kabbalists from Moisés de León to Abraham Abulafia and Isaac Luria envisioned the universe as created by God through words. For them words preceded nature. Words were the purveyor's layout, the master plan.

VA: The Bible has spawned an impressive number of dictionaries. Might we also say that dictionaries have spawned an impressive number of bibles?

IS: In my view, some dictionaries—like the *OED*—are bibles.

VA: Are they sacred?

IS: They surely are.

VA: As you discovered in *Dictionary Days* when you looked at the ignominious definitions of *día* in María Moliner and the *Diccionario de la lengua española* (*DRAE*) of the Real Academia Española, the *DRAE* defines *day* as: "*Tiempo que el Sol emplea en dar, aparentemente, una vuelta a la Tierra.*" (The time it takes the Sun to, apparently, circle the Earth.) And Moliner repeats the error albeit using slightly different words. Lexicographers have always been accusing each other of plagiarism. In 1986 Fredric Dolezal suggested that rather than saying that dictionaries are the result of a sequence of clever and not-so-clever plagiarists, it would help if we indeed viewed the English dictionary as a single text; then the different "authors" of the successive dictionaries would more felicitously be called "editors."

IS: That is a concept put forth by the eighteenth-century thinker Emanuel Swedenborg and emphasized by Ralph Waldo Emerson: the Almighty is the sole Creator, whereas humans are mere scribes. By the way, María Moliner is among the most fascinating cases in the history of female lexicographers.

VA: How so?

IS: Moliner, who died in Madrid in 1981, was a housewife whose energy was committed to recording and cataloguing, by hand, the Spanish "usage." Thus the title *Diccionario* *de uso del español*. It was an extraordinary lexicon released in 1966–1967, immediately applauded by the likes of Miguel Delibes and Gabriel García Márquez. The current edition contains more than three thousand pages and is not only larger but, in my judgment, better that the *DRAE* put forth by the Spanish Academy. Who ever said housewives were wasted?

VA: In a polyglot dictionary published in Paris in 1548 by Pasquier Le Tellier, he included words for intimate functions of the human body—in eight languages! Even staid Dr. Johnson has a six-line poem (by Jonathan Swift) to illustrate "fart" in his dictionary: "to fart. To break wind behind. As when we gun discharge, Although the bore be ne're so large, Before the flame from muzzle burst, Just at the breech it flashes first; So from my lord his passion broke, He farted first, and then he spoke." In *Dictionary Days* you comment on the puritanical aspects of modern dictionaries. What have you found?

IS. That the prudishness is embarrassing. Take the word "fuck." For decades it has been the most used—and abused—monosyllabic term in the English language. Yet only under R.W. Burchfield, chief editor of the *OED* from 1971 to 1984, with a mission to register "offensive parlance" under the radar of the Oxford dons, did the expression make it to the lexicon. In my 1971 edition, for instance, it is absent, believe it or not.

VA: We cannot expect general-purpose monolingual dictionaries to be so all-encompassing that they turn into encyclopedias. However, when I read the definition of "*judío*" in the 2003 edition of the *Diccionario de la lengua española*, and compare it to its definition of "*moro*," I find marked differences in their treatment. The Jewish presence in the Iberian peninsula spans from the second century CE through March 31, 1492—yet no mention of this twelve-century presence or forced departure appears in the definition. In comparison, the Islamic presence spans eight centuries, from 711 CE through the expulsion of the Mozárabes by Isabella on February 11, 1502. The definition of *moro*, however, does include historical information regarding their arrival in Spain and their forced departure—although its historicity is not perfect, for, if we are to be precise, they were expelled in the sixteenth century, not in the fifteenth as stated in the definition. Do lexicographers (and in this case, the Real Academia proper) have special responsibilities when it comes to encyclopedicity regarding definitions pertaining to their own history?

IS: They surely have. A lexicon is a map of its nation's psyche. Lexicographers have a responsibility to describe historical tides.

VA: Ah, the Academy. Over the last few years you've clashed with the Real Academia. Jean Cocteau said: "The trouble about the *Académie* is that by the time they get around to electing us to a seat, we really need a bed." What is the role of these institutions?

IS: Academies are designed to be the authority on language. The function of authority is complex, of course. It records and catalogues. But should an academy also prescribe? I believe in correctness but not when it is achieved through coercion or when it limits freedom.

VA: The *Diccionario de la lengua (DRAE)*, released in 2003, because of its haphazard encyclopedicity and rudimentary scientificity, tells us that a *pantera* is the same as a *leopardo*. To my merriment, Merriam-Webster's Collegiate defines *panther* as "a. A leopard of a hypothetical exceptionally large fierce variety, b. A leopard of the black color phase, 2. Cougar; 3. Jaguar." Furthermore, both dictionaries refuse to tell us where we may encounter panthers, whether as panthers or dressed as leopards, cougars, or jaguars; rather irresponsible on their part. Unless, of course, the beasts' fierceness is indeed hypothetical, their size not worth mentioning, and that black phase they're going through, well, it is just a phase. When I asked the people of the *Diccionario* what a *tinge* was, they got angry at me, Ilan, and shouted: Gosh, woman, what a question! Everyone knows that a *tinge* is "An owl that is stronger and larger than the common one" (*Búho mayor y más fuerte que el común*). This definition brought to mind Kersey's *New Dictionary* (1702) where he defined "dog" as "a beast" and his *Dictionnarium Anglo-Britannicum* (1708), where he simply defines it as "a well-known creature." Lexicographers, it seems, have a very hard time defining animals. You've noticed quite a number of peculiarities in dictionary definitions of animals. What intrigued you about the *OED*'s encyclopedicity when it comes to animals?

IS: The *OED* defines "zebra" as "a South African equine quadruped (Equus or Hippotigris Zebra), of whitish ground-colour stripped all over with regular bars of black, inhabiting mountainous regions, and noted for its wildness and swiftness." But is it "whitish ground-colour" with black stripes or blackish-ground color with white stripes, as other dictionaries put it? It is all in the eye of the beholder. Yet that beholder is partial, subjective, biased...Is a white-based "equine" less threatening than a black-based one?

VA: If you were asked to produce the smallest virtual lexicon ever, a vademecum for the eternally busy reader of today, capable of being transported in a Palm Pilot, what would it contain?

IS: The vademecum (from the Latin "go with me," a word that originated in the seventeenth century) would list words whose definitions would change depending on the date you access it. That, I suspect, is the model of the lexicons of tomorrow: instantly mutating vocabularies.

VA: Would names change too?

IS: With a few exceptions, such as *Collins*, lexicons—unless expressly devoted to toponimy and onomastics—refuse to include names.

VA: Yet names are identity cards. For instance, when Alice asked, "Must a name mean something?" Humpty Dumpty answered with a short laugh "Of course it must. My name means the shape I am—and a good, handsome shape it is, too. With a name like yours, you might be any shape, almost."

IS: Yes, names become things and vice versa, especially with people. People's characters are collapsed into platonic categories instantly organized in our mind. Do all the Johns you know have something in common, to such degree that the word *John* becomes an archetype? The answer is yes, although subjectively. John for me is attached to slim, serious, blond, spectacled individuals, who tend to be too formal. This is because I've synthesized all the Johns I've come across. The same with Jeremy, Brigitte, Antonio, and Olivia. Of course, every so often a John will break the pattern, which, of course, simply proves that such a pattern does exist. And my archetype of John will be different from yours because you've met Johns I'm unacquainted with and vice versa. Are all Alices like the *Alice in Wonderland*? Of course not, but Lewis Carroll's Alice predisposes us to find similes.

VA: Some horses, whether real or imagined, have made their mark in history. There's Robert E. Lee's *Traveller,* George Washington's *Nelson,* Alexander's *Bucephalus,* Don Quixote's *Rocinante,* Caligula's *Incitatus,* Napoleon's *Marengo*...But there's one that piques my curiosity: the Cid Campeador's *Babieca.* I don't know about you, but I picture Rodrigo as a *macho de pelo en pecho* riding a powerful stallion across the Spanish plains. What do you make of his horse's rather inane name?

IS: And let's not forget Bellerophon's *Pegasus,* Reinaldos of Montalván's *Bayard,* and Ruggiero's *Frontino.* In any event, Babieca is an emblematic name and it has a curious mythological past. It isn't until the second *Cantar* of the *Poema de Mío Cid* that *Babieca* makes an appearance. Like the manuscript of Don Quixote, which Cervantes's narrator buys in Toledo and is supposedly in Arabic, Rodrigo Díaz de Vivar—the Campeador—acquires *Babieca* from the emir of Seville, although there are some legends that claim the horse was from León. Yakov Malkiel, whose philological work has opened our eyes to the Hebraic roots of medieval Iberian culture, suggested that *Babieca* is a nickname probably meaning *"el baboso,"* a dumbo. The equivalent practice nowadays, I assume, might be found in the way car companies name their products: Cherokee, Explorer, Touareg, etc.

VA: In 2004 the British Council conducted a survey (it sampled forty thousand) amongst English-language students in forty-six countries and asked them what they thought were the most beautiful words in the English language. According to the results, non-English-speakers voted the following ten words as the most beautiful: (1) mother, (2) passion, (3) smile, (4) love, (5) eternity, (6) fantastic, (7) destiny, (8) freedom, (9) liberty, and (10) tranquility. What do you think of this survey's responses?

IS: I find the list a cliché. Since there are no forty-six countries in the world where English is the English of daily activity, that would explain the inclusion of words like "passion," "smile," and "love." There is the fact that "mother" is #1 but "father" is absent altogether. Is this because *"madre sólo hay una,"* as the Mexican saying goes, but anyone can be a father? Then there is the difference, about which we've talked already in reference to Isaiah Berlin, between "freedom" and "liberty." The inclusion of these two terms on the list is especially conspicuous, since few languages outside of Russian, Polish, English—and perhaps Hebrew—make a distinction between these two concepts. And what is the adjective "fantastic" doing in the list? And "tranquility"? Is there a feminine aspect to the list, by the way? And are these "the most beautiful words in the English language" or are they the words about the most beautiful things in the language? I suspect it's the latter. In terms of beautiful words, I vote for "moon," "wolverine," "anaphora," and "precocious."

VA: Regarding "love," you mentioned in *Dictionary Days* that Acadians, Caldeans, Phoenicians, Sumerians, Babylonians, Egyptians, Normans, Toltecs, Vikings, and Quechuas didn't have a word for it. Knowing that images are an important part of how you see the world, what would you have done had you been born speaking Latin, that according to linguists doesn't have a lexeme for *gray* or *brown*, or born to that of the Dani of New Guinea, whose only color words are for black and white, or speaking a four-color language like Hanunóo that has words only for black, white, green, and red?

IS: The limits of our language are the limits of our worldview.

VA: In *Dictionary Days* you state that there are English words you dislike, amongst them "here" and "now." Yet, terms pertaining to space and time are ubiquitous in English, our borrowed language, because the culture of which we now partake measures its history in time-lines and time frames, its pace in New York minutes, its inventorying in FIFO or LIFO, its production line must run like clockwork, its products delivered in just-in-time and time-to-market frameworks, its manpower is measured in man-hours and clock-hours, its academics in credit-hours...and we all live under the pressure of deadlines and due dates and such. In short, we live by the here and now and the don't-be-late-tomorrows. How have you managed to avoid the "heres" and "nows" in your writing when most of your writing is in English?

IS: My strategy has been to let the reader infer these words. The act of reading takes place in an eternal present. Why reemphasize the time frame in the text? Now that I'm thinking about it, my allergy to these coordinates might be linked to the obsession with them by the Mexican middle class: when people are anxious about their economic and cultural status, they stress the need to enjoy the "here and now," which is what I used to hear, among relatives and friends, all the time. I, for one, don't want to limit my bet to the present. The past and the future are far more important tenses for me.

VA: A few years ago I learned a lovely word, "noumenon."

IS: It comes from Kantian philosophy and implies the impossibility of knowing things as they actually are, for they are not experienced through any of the five senses. Human experience filters everything, and in so doing, it perverts the universe. But that perversion is who we are and, as such, is beautiful.

VA: Love, for instance, is a noumenon, yet its name is absent in many languages. You have a beautiful chapter in *Dictionary Days* about the definition of "love" in Russian, German, Italian, Spanish, and English dictionaries. By the way, do you like the world "beautiful"?

IS: Not particularly.

VA: Having talked about English words that you dislike, I would now like to bring up Spanish words that you're fond of. In particular, I've noticed your attraction to *"rascuache"* and *"rascuachismo."*

IS: These words denote taste as it is defined by class. *"Rascuache"* is an esthetic experience filtered through the eyes of the have-nots. If everything we do is defined by who we are, class—along with religion, politics, and ethnicity—is one of the circumstances shaping our worldview. I fell in love with the concept of *Rascuache* when I moved to the United States, in the mid-1980s, and quickly found out that *"lo mexicano,"* things Mexican, were considered, in the cultural arena, of low quality. Yet, I was shaped by this weltanschauung. Was I therefore inferior? *"Rascuachismo,"* it follows, is a political stand through which the have-nots affirm their worldview. The have-nots often suffer from an inferiority complex but only in the eyes of the cultural elite. Their life, in their own perception, is meaningful.

VA: A few days ago, my doorbell rang. When I picked up the intercom and asked, "Who is it?," I got a very Mexican response: *"No, si no es nadie, Vero, nomás soy yo."* (No, it's no one, Vero, it's just me.) I noticed that in *Dictionary Days* you mention the word *donnadie*: a nobody. And then there is another Mexicanism: *ningunear*.

IS: A verb denoting the act—and art—of turning someone into a nobody. Octavio Paz, in *The Labyrinth of Solitude*, makes a deal out of this lack of self. Yet, does it mean that Mexicans have no self-esteem? Only when people from opposing social statuses interact does it come into play. I have never heard a poor Mexican saying *"no soy nadie"* to a peer. Needless to say, the behavior is universal: I've seen Italians, French, and Germans *ningunearse*, ignoring or making less of one another. In the Middle East, it is a most common activity: Jews giving the back to Palestinians and vice versa. It is sheer Mexican genius to have come with a term for it: *ningunear*. Another Mexicanism I adore is *engentar*, to oversaturate oneself with people, that is, to be "peopled out."

VA: *Bartlett's Roget's Thesaurus*, published in 1996, within its conceptual categories of synonyms, includes many lists of types of things, among them a lengthy list of phobias. Interestingly, there is "logophobia," but there isn't a phobia listed for fearing dictionaries.

IS: Should it be called "lexicophobia"?

VA: Have you ever come across someone suffering from it?

IS: Oh, thousands and thousands. How often does one come across a student who thinks looking up a term in the dictionary is a form of torture? Maybe we should establish a jail system in which inmates are forced to memorize definitions from dictionaries. Depending on the severity of the crime, one would need to memorize two thousand, fifty thousand, one hundred thousand.

VA: In your essay "Gladys," part of *Dictionary Days,* you mentioned a gift you gave to the Salvadoran immigrant that is your protagonist.

IS: It was a pocket-size dictionary.

VA: Did she appreciate it?

IS: Lexicons for Gladys are objects from outer space. She didn't even complete third grade. But as a self-taught woman with little time to spare, she tries to compensate for her limited knowledge with spontaneous efforts at reading. Last time I saw the dictionary, it looked as if it was in constant use.

VA: Even though the first thing she looked for in it was her name and couldn't find it?

IS: Her effort reminded me of a scene in Flaubert's "A Simple Heart" in which the female protagonist, also unschooled, is shown a portion of a map to explain where someone she loves has moved to. What does the protagonist do? She looks for the actual person in the map.

VA: At the *Congreso Internacional de Historia de la Lengua Española* in Zacatecas in 1997, Gabriel García Márquez caused a ruckus when he proposed simplifying Spanish orthography. There have been numerous proposals to do the same to English spelling, and there is even a Simplified Spelling

Society in the United States. German-speaking countries signed an agreement in 1996 for a major spelling reform, and a new recommended orthography, albeit limited, has been adopted by Belgium, France, and Quebec. What are your views on spelling reform?

IS: Even though orthography is somehow an invitation to look at words from a historical perspective—to trace their etymology—I'm in favor of spelling reform, particularly in Spanish. Andrés Bello, the Antonio de Nebrija of the Americas and one of the most illustrious thinkers in the Hispanic world, made a solid orthographic proposal in the nineteenth century, but only a minuscule fraction of his recommendations were implemented. Diacritics, the difference between s, c, and z, as well as b and v, the silent h, are in need of reexamination. Globalism should be an invitation to look at language anew. The use of language in the Internet, in particular, begs for simplification. But simplification should not be confused with stupidity: to simplify an orthography isn't the same as designing a language for idiots only.

VA: Riddling is an intellectual game that is found in many cultures, in all continents, and throughout history. But riddling is not universal. Pukapuka is the most isolated island in the Cooks group and was immortalized by the American writer Robert Dean Frisbie in his books *The Book of Puka Puka* and *The Island of Desire*. But, according to linguist David Crystal, in Pukapuka and in Manus in the Admiralty Islands, you would not be able to play *Lotería*. Neither could you play it with the Miao of China. What attracted you to explore riddling?

IS: Riddles and tongue-twisters are favorite pastimes of mine. I'm not a poet but I love building these linguistic structures, among other reasons because they allow us to be challenged by randomness. The *lotería* is a game of random and language, which, although standardized, is also defined by randomness: what we say and how we say it is decided by the climate, the time of day, our mood...Isaiah, my eight-year-old, recited this tongue-twister yesterday:

> Whether the weather is fine,
> or whether the weather is not.
> Whether the weather is cold,
> or whether the weather is hot.
> We weather the weather,
> whatever the weather,
> whether we like it or not.

VA: What is your favorite tongue-twister in Spanish?

IS: How about this one?

> Si tu gusto gustara del gusto
> que gusta mi gusto,
> mi gusto gustaría del gusto
> que gusta tu gusto.
> Pero como tu gusto
> no gusta del gusto
> que gusta mi gusto,
> mi gusto no gusta del gusto
> que gusta tu gusto.

VA: What linguistic internal resources do you think monolingual people must tap in order to express the multiple aspects of their personality?

IS: Monolinguals are imprisoned in a single-channeled existence. Imagine having a radio capable of broadcasting only a single channel. Or else, buying clothes at a store selling only black garments.

VA: Living in two or more cultures, two or more languages, produces some rifts and upheavals; it requires a constant rearranging of schemata. According to Eliezer Nowodworski, among those who attempt to overcome this cultural schizophrenia, even make money out of it, are translators. Nowodworski is fond of saying that translation is neither a profession nor a trade, not even a calling, but rather a pathology. You have written extensively on life on the hyphen in *The Essential Ilan Stavans*. In the same volume you also have essays on translation per se. Is translation a pathology?

IS: I wouldn't describe it as such. Translation is an essential human activity, older than the archetypical Tower of Babel. In the Bible, the moment God communicates with Adam and Eve in Genesis 1:1, an act of translation takes place building a bridge between the *"lashon ha-kodesh,"* the divine language, and the *"lashon bnei adam,"* the language of humankind. Translation is everywhere: on the movie screen, in the classroom, in the doctor's office, among lovers . . . Of course, translators are prone to become obsessed with their endeavor. But there is most joy, even spontaneity, in the activity. Furthermore, translation always involves wonderment and surprise: what is the speaker really saying? Is there a way to convey the message in my own language? Is it possible to avoid becoming a falsifier? The answer to the last question, obviously, is no. Every translation is a misrepresentation.

VA: In 1963 Bishop John Robinson's *Honest to God* became a national best-seller with over a million copies sold. Robinson argued that theologians, when speaking about God, use terminology that distances God from the believers. He questioned the tradition of using either highly abstract and mystical terms such as *Infinite One, The Unknowable*, and crude spatial metaphors as if He *were up there* or *out there*. The book argued that, to contemporary audiences, such language was outmoded. Several experiments in religious communication followed the publication of his book and a new academic discipline, *theography*, was proposed. Its aim was to "draw a map" of the language that people use to talk about God. Is this proposed theography an academic utopia, or is it a dystopia? As Nowodworski has phrased it, would the concept of God, in a place like New York City— with its plurality of languages and creeds—be the same in Washington Heights, in The Village, or in Murray Hill?

IS: Isaac Luria, a kabbalist in Safed in the sixteenth century, said that all names for the divine are subterfuges. For God is beyond human language. But, of course, what other recourse do we have to address the higher powers that surround and overwhelm us other than our imperfect human language? And human languages are shaped by their users. So the divine in Oslo, Lublin, and San José is different as is its appellation.

CHAPTER SEVEN

Libraries

I have always imagined that Paradise will be a kind of library.
—Jorge Luis Borges

Verónica Albin: In the past, you've defined the term "word" as "the fabric we use to dress our thoughts." What is a "book," then?

Ilan Stavans: I've seen analogies between books and bombs, tombs, pharmacies, wineries, and grocery stores. For me a book is a closet where all sorts of customs are stored. It is left to us to pick and choose.

VA: The metaphor of the closet is often used these days, but I had never heard it in relation to the library.

IS: Our present culture gives the impression of moving swiftly away from the printed word. Enter an airport and what do you see? Graphic signs for exits, baggage claim, car rentals, toilets, information. These days it is possible to be monolingual and illiterate and travel from Buenos Aires to Mumbai without obstacle. But the printed word remains the means for traveling, not longitudinally, but through time. Language survives only in books. It is fixed for future generations.

VA: Most of what goes on in life doesn't make it into books though.

IS: Mercifully...Books should discriminate. And when approaching books, readers should also be choosy. According to the Bowker Annual, in 2003 there were approximately 190,000 books published in the United States alone. What on earth could they contain? The vast majority doesn't deserve a place in the library; they belong in the trash dump. Take self-help manuals: their purpose is to make the reader feel good in the here and now. Good books never do that; they are always skeptical of the present.

VA: And "library," how should the word be defined?

IS: Ay, ay, ay...It is a bazaar of ideas, a portal to alternative dimensions, and a space of absolute openness. In the dead of night, when no one is around, I believe books in a library forsake their order, jump out of their shelves, and dance around in order to chat and gossip with one another...I imagine pages ceding from their original binding and inserting themselves between other pages in other covers. Were they to meet, what would Spinoza and Machiavelli talk about? Karl Marx and Oscar Wilde? Langston Hughes and Marina Tsvetaeva? It is a scene reminiscent of Jonathan Swift's "Battle of the Books," of the melee he imagined in 1710 in the library in St. James, except that in my vision there is less of a fight and more of eroticism. Volumes penetrate one another. They toss and turn as they come in contact with their kin.

VA: Ay, ay, ay is right. Let's get back on safe ground, at least for a little while. I like the reference to the bazaar. Today libraries are market-oriented.

IS: In the United States, in order to justify the public money they depend on, they have to do everything in their power to bring in bodies, even if those bodies aren't interested in reading. And so they improvise themselves as classrooms, theaters, exhibit areas, lecture halls, play-rooms, shopping areas...

VA: Shopping areas?

IS: Just as in the case of museums, in places like the New York Public Library, the store is an essential destination. In a consumer society like ours, this trend is inevitable. Art for art's sake is redundant. So is literature for litera-ture's sake. In order to be worthy, a book has to sell.

VA: We often hear of the decline in reading among the young. Do you agree?

IS: I don't. Reading is a solitary activity. It is also elitist.

VA: Antidemocratic?

IS: No, reading has always been the endeavor of a small, open-minded group of people. There is no need to expand the size of it. Again, success in literature has nothing to do with sales. A good book is a good book even if it only has a couple of readers.

VA: Does that elite include politicians?

IS: Seldom...I have little patience for politicians. My vision of a utopian future excludes them altogether. Yes, just like Plato did to the poets I would do to politicians: make their profession irrelevant.

VA: Is that possible?

IS: Probably not, but this isn't reason enough to stop hoping. At the very least, the model should be Denmark, not the United States.

VA: How so?

IS: Do you know the name of Switzerland's prime minister?

VA: I don't.

IS: Neither do I. In truth, I don't even know if the country has a president or a prime minister. That, to me, is a triumph. In America there is an obnoxious cult of political personality, which dates back to the founding fathers. Do we need to know every single detail about Thomas Jefferson's life, what he ate for breakfast, what he thought about agriculture, etc.? That idol worship extends to current presidents and, to a lesser extent, cabinet members. George W. Bush strikes me as a rather insignificant individual, one with whom I wouldn't spend even half an hour. Bill Clinton was slightly more interesting, but not enough to justify a dinner. Anonymity, I'm convinced, is best for politics.

VA: And for literature? Would you be as prolific if your name didn't appear in book covers?

IS: I would be. Yes, anonymity is also recommendable for literature.

VA: You're well-known for your eloquent meditations on dictionaries. Is there an analogy between dictionaries and libraries?

IS: Like dictionaries, libraries have concealed information from the public. Think of erotica. Should it have a prominent place in them? As a grad student at Columbia University, I always chuckled while browsing through the periodical section of Butler Library, wondering why there was no subscription to *Playboy*. For better or for worse, isn't the magazine a record of our dreams? What makes it less useful than say *The Onion*? Aside from the photographs, it is famous for its in-depth interviews. Shouldn't students have access to this kind of magazine? In other words, libraries, like dictionaries, not only reveal information, they also hide it from their readers. The question of granting *Playboy* a place in Butler makes me think of Henry Spencer Ashbee, the nineteenth-century English collector of erotica. Like Sir Richard Francis Burton, he sought to rethink the Victorian code of morality—with limited success. Ashbee is also known as the possible author (known as "Walter") of *My Secret Life*, first published in 1888 and banned in England and the United States for years. It was only in 1966 that Grove Press published it. He also collected *Don Quixotes*. When the British Library came looking for a donation of the latter, he complied, but only on the condition that his erotica also made it to the stacks.

VA: It was reluctantly received, for it stayed for years hidden in the Private Case Collection and out of the *General Catalogue* and thus out of reach for most everyone.

IS: Yes, up until 1965 Ashbee's collection, as well as the rest of the erotica held by the British Library, was available only to the institution's staff and to those with contacts in high places. But forty years later the staff is still uncomfortable when anybody asks to see these volumes, for they sure ask a lot of questions before calling these books from the stacks.

VA: Has a library ever been turned into the protagonist of a novel?

IS: Jorge Luis Borges, of course, made the library a centerpiece of his oeuvre. Umberto Eco, in turn, put Borges inside a library in his thriller *The Name of the Rose*. These are only two references, though. Think of Sor Juana Inés de la Cruz and Shakespeare, Heinrich Heine and Elias Canetti, Avicenna and Walter Benjamin, Edward Gibbon and the Umayyads . . . and libraries are prominent in *Don Quixote* and, not surprisingly, given his tenure as assistant librarian, in Swift's *Gulliver's Travels*. And we must not forget Rabelais, where his *Pantagruel* visits the library of Saint Victor's in Paris, and Poe, who spiced his stories with quotes from a nonexistent library. One of the most erudite and entertaining reference volumes on the topic is Alberto Manguel's *A History of Reading*. (Its title is a take on Borges's *A Universal History of Infamy*.)

VA: How did your love affair with books begin?

IS: I wasn't a bookish child. Instead, I loved the outdoors: hiking, camping, playing sports...Soccer was my passion. I rooted for *El América*, a wealthy team owned by Televisa, the equivalent to Manchester United in the British League. I didn't begin reading in earnest until I was in my late teens.

VA: Which of your books do you cherish the most?

IS: In Mexico I was an assiduous book buyer. Public libraries were a disaster: ill-equipped, atrociously managed. I remember using, on occasion, the one at the *Centro Deportivo Israelita*. But mostly I bought books. The moment I fell in love with books, the romance was profound. And it was quite possessive, too. I needed to own everything I read: Hermann Hesse, Rabindranath Tagore, Sholem Asch, Pearl S. Buck...I lived in Copilco, in the southern parts of Mexico City. The Librería Gandhi opened sometime in the 1970s. It was owned by a Jew whose family was into trade and manufacturing. He was a rebel, interested in intellectual, not in material, culture. I remember the business when it was still in its incipient stages; it was a veritable marketplace of ideas that catered to a middle-class esthetic. I remember reading literary supplements such as *Sábado*, edited by Huberto Batis and published by the newspaper *Unomásuno*. I remember running to "La Gandhi" to acquire the latest book I had read about: *The Magic Mountain* by Thomas Mann, *The Moonstone* by Wilkie Collins...*Red Cavalry* by Isaac Babel. Has anyone ever studied the intellectual impact of a bookstore on a generation? La Gandhi was a bridge between Mexico and the outside world. It made us less nearsighted, more cosmopolitan. Over time, the books began to overwhelm the bookshelves I made at home. So I built more. When I moved to New York City in 1985, I brought with me only a small amount. I remember agonizing over the list: which volumes should accompany me on my next stage in life?

VA: The first chapter of *On Borrowed Words* is a lyrical description of that turning point. You even offer a list of the titles you chose to bring with you: Joyce, Kafka, Flaubert...

IS: Ironically, I never reopened most of them again—at least not those in translation. They were my companions for years. But my northbound migration was also a journey into different languages. Why read *Portrait of the Artist as a Young Man* in Spanish if one is able to access it in the original? In subsequent travels I availed myself of copies of *Madame Bovary* in French, *Tevye the Dairyman* in Yiddish, the *Divine Comedy* in Italian, *The Scarlet Letter* in English... Again, I began to accumulate volumes. Somehow I believed that possessing books was a statement of identity. My personal library needed to be not only multifarious, but chaotic. Yes, chaotic. I've always admired people able to organize their books. It doesn't come easy to me. The universe is in a permanent disorder, as is—or better, it was for a long time—my library. It came to the point that I didn't know how many books I owned. Worse, I didn't know where I had them. In my home in Amherst, Massachusetts, I had over ten thousand volumes. I ought to be honest: I was inspired by them but also overwhelmed. They took much space, externally and inside my mind. Then, in early 2005, a close friend of mine died a tragic death. He was in his early seventies, overweight, a chain-smoker, absolutely careless about his diet. He suffered an aneurism. One of his legs needed to be amputated. He was semiconscious in the hospital for a couple of weeks. He and I had had a falling out some months before and didn't have time to make peace with one another. His passing was traumatic. In order to cleanse myself, I abruptly decided to organize my library. But no sooner did I embark on the task, I paid attention to something my wife Alison had been telling me for a long time: with an outstanding library a couple of blocks away from our house, and ready access to the Internet everywhere, did I really need to own all those books? I suddenly made a choice: I would donate four thousand volumes to the library, and two thousand more to launch a special collection devoted to two fields: Jewish–Hispanic relations and Latino culture in the United States. I still have around four thousand left. These are my most precious items: a comprehensive collection of *Borgeana* of around seven hundred items, another one, twice the size, of dictionaries and lexicography, and a library of translations of *Don Quixote of La Mancha* into a good number of languages.

VA: You seem obsessed with language.

IS: Of all the obsessions I might think of, this one is rather harmless. It is a gentle madness that doesn't really bother anyone. Nor does it make you sick. Plus, and it is a plus, it is also all-encompassing. To be obsessed with language is to be obsessed with the universe. Dr. Johnson once said:

> My zeal for language may seem, perhaps, rather overheated, even to those by whom I desire to be well esteemed. To those who have nothing in their thoughts but trade or policy, present power or present money, I should not think it necessary to defend my opinions; but with men of letters I would not unwillingly compound, by wishing the continuance of every language, however narrow in its extent, or however incommodious for common purposes, till it is reposited in some version of a known book, that it may be always hereafter examined and compared with other languages, and then permitting its disuse.

VA: In *On Borrowed Words*, there is a crucial scene in which you make a bonfire with your own books. I quote from pages seven and eight:

> When I began to write, Borges had a decisive influence. His pure, precise, almost mathematical style; his intelligent plots; his abhorrence of *verborrea*—the overflow of words without rhyme or reason, still a common malady in Spanish literature today. He, more than anyone before him (including the *modernista* poet from Nicaragua, Rubén Darío), had taught us a lesson: literature ought to be a conduit for ideas. But his lesson was hard to absorb, if only because Hispanic civilization is so unconcerned with ideas, so irritable about debate, so uninterested in systematic inquiry. Life is too rough, too unfinished to be wasted on philosophical disquisition. It is not by chance,

of course, that Borges was an Argentine. It couldn't have
been otherwise, for Argentina perceives itself—or rather,
it *used to* perceive itself—as a European enclave in the
Southern Hemisphere. Buenos Aires, its citizens would
tell you in the 1940s, is the capital of the world, with Paris
as a provincial second best.

As soon as I discovered Borges, I realized, much as
others have, that I had to own him. I acquired every edition I could put my hands on, not only in Spanish but
in their French, English, Italian, German, and Hebrew
translations, as well as copies of the Argentine monthly
Sur, where his best work was originally featured, and all
his interviews in journals. My collection began to grow
as I embarked on my own first experiences in literature: tight descriptions, brief stories, passionless literary
essays. Rather quickly the influence he exerted on me
became obvious. In consolation, I would paraphrase for
myself the famous line from "Decalogue of the Perfect
Storyteller"—in Spanish its title is infinitely better:
"Decálogo del perfecto cuentista"—by Horacio Quiroga, a
celebrated, if tragic, turn of the century Uruguayan
author: to be born, a young writer should *imitate* his
beloved masters as much as possible. The maxim, I realize today, is not without dangerous implications; it has
encouraged derivativeness and perhaps even plagiarism in
Latin American letters. But I was blind to such views. My
only hope as a litterateur was not to be like Borges, but to
be Borges. How absurd that sounds now!

Influence turned into anxiety, and anxiety into
discomfort. Would I ever have my own voice? One
desperate afternoon, incapable of writing a single line
I could call my own, I brought down all the Borges titles

I owned, piled them in the garage, poured gasoline over them, and set them on fire. It was a form of revenge, a sacramental act of desperation: the struggle to be born, to own a place of one's own, to be like no one else—or, at least, unlike Borges. The flames shot up at first, and eventually, slowly, died down. I saw the volumes, between fifty and seventy in total, turn bright, then brown, then turn to ash. I smiled, thinking, in embarrassment, of Hitler's Germany, Pinochet's Chile, and Mao's China. I thought of Elias Canetti's *Auto da Fé* and Ray Bradbury's *Fahrenheit 451*. I thought of scores of prayer books, Talmuds, and other rabbinical works burnt by the Holy Inquisition in Spain and the New World, in places not far from my home. And I also invoked Borges's own essay, "The Wall and the Books," about Shih Huang Ti, the first emperor of China, a contemporary of Hannibal, whose reign was marked by the construction of the Wall of China, and also by the campaign to burn all history books. Shih Huang Ti saw himself as a new beginning. History needed to start over.

IS: It was a rite of passage, although it doesn't make me less embarrassed.

VA: Did you ever consider becoming a librarian?

IS: Yes. And a rabbi too. And a grave-digger.

VA: I can't possibly let this answer drop. Why a grave-digger, of all occupations?

IS: Perhaps because I love silence ... As it happens, the only place where I don't enjoy silence is in libraries.

VA: Why?

IS: It makes me uncomfortable. Why should we be quiet next to books? Shouldn't it be the other way around? Does the human brain function better in quiet? I'm not convinced...

VA: The way a personal library is arranged, you state in *Dictionary Days*, is a key to deciphering the owner's character.

IS: And temperament, too. Reason is our response to nature, just like order is a response to chaos. Recently, I've been interested in the history of libraries. The library of the city of Nineveh, Mesopotamia, around the seventh century BCE contained books made of clay. The dream of building a repository devoted to every book imaginable belongs to Alexandria in the first century CE. Its library is rumored to have contained Aristotle's personal collection (although it is also said that the collection was buried in a hole in Athens). It was the site were Ptolemeic philosophy flourished: Euclid, Strabo, and Galen; and the *Septuaginta*, for example, the translation of the Torah into Greek, was produced there.

VA: How did the libraries in antiquity order their scrolls?

IS: Mostly in a haphazard fashion, in piles according to author and geographical coordinates (Egyptian, Biblical, Early Catholic, Hellenistic, Byzantine, etc.). The Alexandria collection showcased papyri rapped with a peg called *umbilicus*, announcing the author and title. The thematic order belongs to the Napoleonic age, a time when the French embarked on colonial ventures to Africa and the East and returned with a plethora of artifacts. Cataloguing these artifacts required thought. The artifacts also needed a place to be displayed. In response, the museum, as it is conceived today—that is, a series of thematically related galleries—was implemented. The Biblioteca Apostolica Vaticana was structured within a room full of tables. On the left, *aka* the sinister side, were books on apostasy, heresy, alchemy, and the profane. On the right, the dexter side, were the righteous books on heavenly themes. Other libraries, due to economy of space, organized the books according to size and thickness. Some sense of order, however remote, was implemented; otherwise, the library would be…well, unreasonable. I guess my point is that libraries have specific metabolisms, and it is those that need to be read as well.

VA: How about borrowing books?

IS: It is also a rather recent phenomenon. Books today are, to a large extent, produced in large numbers. This is the result of the invention not only of movable print but, in the early part of the twentieth century, of the hard-cover and paperback formats. Thus, the same novel is available in scores of libraries these days. In ancient times, copies of books were scarce. The copyist did everything by hand, patiently. Errors crept in, which meant that each copy was unique. Libraries stored individual copies and readers read them within the premises. The concept of book-borrowing is linked to the rise of a populist understanding of society. At its core was the principle that class shouldn't be an obstacle; the haves and have-nots should have an equal piece of it. This revolution had a profound effect on society.

VA: How so?

IS: Up until the late nineteenth century, writers in the West were, predominantly, members of the upper crust. In our age, literature is the domain of the middle-class.

VA: Should we trust librarians?

IS: I'm not sure the word "trust" is right. I believe skepticism is the best approach to knowledge. Not too long ago, I published the four-volume *Encyclopedia Latina*, a work of reference on Hispanic culture in the United States. It was a monumental project: a million and a half words, almost seven hundred entries, with more than three hundred contributors from an array of countries. Do you know what aspect of it I enjoyed the most? Not the actual editing, which sucked; nor the writing itself, which became mechanical. The most enjoyable aspect for me was the mapping of the encyclopedia. If you were to embark on a reference book on God, where would you start? Or better yet, were would you end? I needed to survey Hispanic culture north of the Rio Grande from beginning to end. That is, it was up to me to establish a beginning and an end. Because I had constraints of time and space, some elements would eventually need to be left out. But which ones? How to make an encyclopedia where the sum of everything that went in it was far superior to that which was left out? Libraries have a similar task: to include the entire universe inside their walls. But how can this be done if the universe always breaches its levees? By means of selection. Most libraries are deliberately selective: they might concentrate on maritime history, food, or art. Their selectiveness might be the result of their users' requests and tastes. What are people in a certain neighborhood where the library is located interested in, for instance? The librarian makes assumptions and establishes parameters in accordance with the library's scope, audience, and budget. Those parameters might be nearsighted for they might allow people to indulge in what they already know. But that is for us to decide. In any case, we should be grateful for librarians, just as we should be thankful for teachers. They aren't generators, but rather facilitators of knowledge.

VA: In other words, libraries aren't politically neutral spaces...

IS: In 2003 my wife and I built a house in Wellfleet, Massachusetts, where the population is known for its literary taste. But what kind of taste? Among the first errands I set for myself was the donation of a handful of my books to the local public library. I gave them the three-volume set of *Isaac Bashevis Singer: Collected Stories* as well as *The Oxford Book of Jewish Stories*. But I also included *The Hispanic Condition* and *Spanglish: The Making of a New American Language*. In searching through the stacks a year later, I discovered that they had only catalogued the books I had written that dealt with Jewish topics. The ones on Latino culture had been deaccessed. I asked the chief librarian why they were no longer in the stacks. Her answer: we know our readership. What she seemed to forget was that even though the majority of house owners and renters are Caucasian with a solid education, the local construction, maintenance, and cleaning crews are Puerto Rican, Brazilian, and Mexican.

VA: Are you implying the librarian is a censor?

IS: She is certainly prudish.

VA: What about current cataloguing systems?

IS: The major revolution we're still defined by was sparked by Melvil Louis Dewey, who actually studied in the institution I've taught at since 1993: Amherst College. He graduated around 1872. While he was here, he found himself dismayed by the disorder of books. So he came up with a decimal classification. But he went far beyond. He was instrumental in the founding of the American Library Association; he went into the office-supply business, and he implemented a new, modern education for librarians. When appreciating his contribution, the key word is efficiency. In this he was an American to the core. In the second half of the nineteenth century, just as the nation was moving into an industrial mode, he devised a strategy to make knowledge more easily manageable. Over time, the Dewey system has been replaced by an array of alternative cataloguing methods, including the one by the Library of Congress, which, since its implementation in the 1970s, has been under heavy artillery attack for being not only bureaucratic but needlessly labyrinthine. It juxtaposes letters and numbers in a maddening fashion: JK216.

T7 1835. It obviously follows a logistical pattern but to me it looks like an alchemic combination. The Library of Congress also uses those subject classes popping up on your screen whenever you select a title: "Democracy—United States—Politics and government—Social conditions." I've come across users describing those classes as nearsighted and racist.

VA: What is your connection to the library at Amherst College?

IS: I love it. I wouldn't have become the person that I am, interested in the humanities, if it wasn't for Frost Library. I spend much time in it. Every so often, I feel Dewey's spirit wandering around the place, appreciating how books are ordered, the reverential attitude students have toward them.

VA: What is the difference between bibliophilia and bibliomania?

IS: Bibliomania is a malady I'm delighted to have overcome, and that is what I had before my friend's death. Believe it or not, reducing the number of books around me has granted me a sense of inner freedom. My mind, I get the sense, is less clotted, more spacious...

VA: Richard de Bury was who coined the term "bibliophile" in the Middle Ages. Have you become a bibliophile?

IS: I was always one, even before I became a passionate reader. And being a passionate reader is more liberating, and thus more rewarding, than being a passionate writer.

VA: In an essay called "The First Book," reprinted in your collection *Art and Anger*, you reminisce about the Torah as a sacred book.

IS: Literature is about pleasure, whereas religion is about fear. Attending synagogue, I am struck by the ritual of getting the Book out of the *aron ha-kodesh,* or Sacred Ark, and onto the people. Each time it happens, the entire congregation is on its toes. The Book, dressed up in beautiful regalia, is paraded around the prayer hall. The faithful rush to kiss it. When I wrote the essay in 1995, I sought to convey the feeling of the transtemporal continuity I sensed in these moments. A decade later, I no longer think quite the same way. It feels as if 9/11 pushed the world to the brink. Everywhere one goes, religion has been emphasized. Not only are Muslims more radical overall, so are Christians and Jews. Look at America: the country is more fearful of God today than it was in the mid-twentieth century. Creationism, *aka* Intelligent Design, has become a force in schools, taught side by side with Evolution...and sometimes replacing it altogether. The text in the Torah is ahistorical; it also has the attribute of perfection. The thought is overwhelming. Whenever I publish a book, I struggle to make it as close to perfect as possible. What do I understand for perfection? The desire to fix it in the best possible way with the capabilities I have at my disposal—talent and technology—at the present time. It will be as free of errors as possible. But if were to reread it, I know that I'll be tempted to improve it, that is, to make it better according to the views I'll have at that time. Whitman kept on rewriting *Leaves of Grass*. At times his revisions improved the text, at others they diminished it. Over time, the book became a record, an accumulation, of Whitman's versions of himself. In the end, it is a human book: perfect in its imperfections. Not the Torah, the Qur'an, and the New Testament, though. Every letter in them, every dot, every empty space has a raison d'être. The Author of Authors is infallible. His existence is a negation of an editorial process. Among the Jews, this approach is expounded by the Kabbalists with particular fervor. The alphabet is a roadmap the Almighty used to create the universe. Before the *Tohu Va-Vohu* of Genesis 1:1, the Hebrew language was already fully formed. Furthermore, the Torah itself was written before Creation, making human affairs but a pale repetition.

VA: What book do you covet the most and would wish to own?

IS: I don't have disposable money to buy antiquarian books. My children are still young and their lives need to be set in motion; for this I need resources. But if I had enough funds I would buy Borgeana. A dealer in Boston often puts on the market holographic manuscripts I am in awe even to contemplate: "Tlön Uqbar Tertius Orbis," an essay on the defeat of Hitler and the end of World War II.

VA: Would you consider yourself a collector?

IS: No doubt. I would become a collector of *Johnsoniana*. Samuel Johnson was a polymath for whom I have enormous admiration. His essays on the English poets, his travel writing with Boswell in Scotland, his *A Dictionary of the English Language*...Another friend, Paul T. Ruxin, a generous Amherst College alum in Chicago, owns such a collection.

VA: Do you think it is bibliophilia or bibliomania that makes Alonso Quijano go mad?

IS: He doesn't quite go mad. Cervantes is careful not to diagnose his protagonist, at least not early on in part one of the novel. He simply tells us that "he fairly lost his wits." That, at least, is the resort English translators often embrace. In Spanish, the reader is told: *"y así, del poco dormir y del mucho leer, se le secó el cerebro de manera que vino a perder el juicio."* In other words, his brains dried up from too much reading and too little sleep. I'm flabbergasted by this image of water. The opposite is also in evidence: too much fantasy "floods" the mind with nonsense? By this medieval conception, the brain is a sponge filled with liquid, which it pours into the environment as a result of excessive behavior. I remember reading a treatise by the eleventh-century ascetic Bahya ben Joseph ibn Paquda (cit. EJ) called *Hovot ha-Levavot* (Book of the Duties of the Heart), written in Arabic and translated into Hebrew by Yehuda ibn Tibbon, in which the author suggests that crying is good for babies because it empties the brain from needless water, which might prevent coherent reasoning. Anyhow, Quixada, or Quesada, starts off as a bibliomaniac. Happily, he ends not as a bibliophile but as an eponymous character in Western literature: an hidalgo described by others as a madman who, in spite of the dryness of his brains, is fully conscious of his role as a fictitious character.

VA: In other words, he knows he lives in a book...

IS: Maybe he is imprisoned in it. By the way, the novel, Cervantes's narrator tells us, was written originally in Arabic. He found the manuscript in Toledo and what we read is a makeshift translation. The topic of translation in *Don Quixote* is essential: it points to the roots of Iberian identity yet it falsifies those roots. In part two, chapter sixty-two, Don Quixote and Sancho Panza, already in Barcelona, enter a printing house. Don Quixote talks to a workman in charge of rendering a book called *Le Bagatelle* (about which we know nothing) from the Italian into Spanish. Don Quixote asks the translator if he has come across the word "piñata" (which Tobias Smollett appropriately spells "*Pignatta*," defined by the *Diccionario de la Real Academia*, in honor of the portly Sancho, as an "*olla panzuda*") and wonders how it should be translated. They start a discussion. Eventually Don Quixote says in P.A. Motteaux's translation:

> Notwithstanding all your learning, I could almost swear you are hitherto unknown to the world, which is ever averse to remunerate flourishing genius, and works of merit. What talents are lost, what abilities obscured, and what virtues are undervalued in this degenerate age! Yet, nevertheless, a translation from one language to another, excepting always those sovereign tongues the Greek and Latin, is, in my opinion, like the wrong

side of a Flemish tapestry, in which, tho' we distinguish
the figures, they are confused and obscured by ends
and threads, without that smoothness and expression
which the other side exhibits: and to translate from easy
languages, argues neither genius nor elocution, nor any
merit superior to that of transcribing from one paper
to another; but, from hence, I would not infer that
translation is not a laudable exercise; for, a man may
employ his time in a much worse and more unprofitable
occupation.

VA: Might *Le Bagatelle* be an invented book?

IS: Perhaps. It is delicious to visit libraries of nonexistent
books. I once went to the one in Sagrurt, Krakozhia,
in the Balkans. The librarian Viktor Navorski gave
us an enlightening tour. I touched a copy of Johann
Valentin Andreä's *Lesbare und lesenswethe Bemerkungen
uber das Land Ukkbar in Klein-Asien*. There were also
two copies, one in English, the other in Sanskrit (the
back cover in poor shape), of *A Modest Defense of the
Proceedings of the Rabble in all Ages*. I found a small bibliography of Guatemalan author Alcina Lubitch Domecq
and a version of *The Mirror's Mirror: Or, Noble Smile of
the Dog* in French. Furthermore, on the second floor,
while the other visitors listened to a lecture, I read a
portion of *Voyage to England, by a Person of Quality in
Terra Australis Incognita*. The experience was not unlike
spending time in the basement, guided by the direc-
tor Werner Gundersheimer, of the Folger Shakespeare
Library in Washington, D.C. He showed me material of

actor David Garrick, a quarto of Shakespeare's *Twelfth Night*.

VA: In the opening line of *Dictionary Days*, your eight-year-old son Isaiah wonders if words die. Let me ask you now, do books die?

IS: A few weeks ago I reread Ray Bradbury's *Fahrenheit 451*, of which François Truffaut made a film adaptation in 1966 with Julie Christie. I had first read it in my twenties, along with *The Martian Chronicles*. It is a rather primitive novel, poorly executed—to use a Truman Capote image, Bradbury didn't as much write it as he typed it. But the message is powerful. Do books die? One hopes they don't but in fact they do. Books are depositories of memory. As such, they are dangerous artifacts. Politicians, not known as promoters of enlightenment, stage rallies to burn them. Books are shunned, banned, discredited, burned. Or else, they drown them in a pool of misconception. (I dream of a future without governments.) But in a capitalist system, books usually die from neglect. This isn't necessarily bad: far too many books aren't worth a dime. The books that matter, though, the ones we cannot do without—and these are just a few thousand—manage to survive. They come back in unpredictable ways, sometimes mutilated, sometimes reincarnated in atrocious adaptations. Sooner or later, they manage to reconfigure themselves. Yet, there is a certain type of magic to the whole phenomenon, for books are intelligent entities. Their survival depends on humane, merciful readers whose task in life is to preserve the ideas they contain.

VA: You just said that "books are depositories of memory." This brings to mind Aby Warburg's eighty-thousand-volume library. As a motto, Warburg had the name of the mother of all the Muses, Mnemosyne, the Goddess of memory, inscribed over the doors of his library.

IS: George Steiner once called Warburg "one of the seminal figures in modern culture." Warburg heard the goose-stepping all right, but he could not do anything about the library. He died by the time the Nazis declared in December 1933 the "Jewish Warburg Library" closed to all, especially to scholars, but he would have been glad to know that the entire library took to sea aboard the *Hermia* and the *Jessica*. It is now part of the University of London. Mnemosyne must have been pleased with Aby's work, for those eighty thousand books live on.

VA: In 1998 one of your stories, "Xerox Man," was broad-casted worldwide by the BBC in London. The protagonist is a book thief, a bibliokleptomaniac.

IS: An Orthodox Jew, Argentine by birth.

VA: He steals Judaica books from rare rooms like the ones at Yale University and The Jewish Theological Seminary.

IS: He then Xeroxes them but always eliminates one page from the photocopied version. The universe is imperfect, he believes. Why shouldn't books mimic than imperfection?

VA: It's a marvelous story. Its central motif is a *genizah*.

IS: The Hebrew word *genizah* means "container," "treasury," "storage," and "archives." Every synagogue has one: the place where sacred texts no longer in use are deposited. Perhaps the most famous one is the Cairo *genizah* of the Ben Ezra Synagogue in Fostat, built in 882 CE. On a trip to Egypt in 1890 two learned Scottish women, Agnes Smith Lewis and Margaret Dunlop Gibson, came across old documents in a bazaar. They immediately recognized the importance of their find, so when they got back to England, they met with Solomon Schechter, a Cambridge professor, and showed him the fragments they had acquired. One of these fragments—in Hebrew—happened to be from the Wisdom of Ben Sira, dating to the tenth century, which until then was solely available in more modern versions in Greek and Syriac. The Hebrew version deposited on Schechter's desk had been lost for approximately a thousand years. The scholar traveled to Cairo, secured access to the documents in the *genizah,* and spent years deciphering some of its 250,000 items, including bills, letters, catalogs, calendars, children's primers, dictionaries, glossaries in Hebrew, Arabic, Coptic, Persian, and even Yiddish...a whole spectrum of Jewish secular material, not only religious life. (Of these, Schechter rescued some 100,000 pieces.) There were also some sixty holographic fragments from Rabbi Moshe ben Maimon, known by his Latin name Maimonides, author of the *Mishna Torah* and the *Guide of the Perplexed*. Maimonides was chief physician to the Egyptian Sultan Saladin and died in Cairo in 1204. In any case, as I've said earlier the Cairo synagogue that housed the *genizah* was built in the ninth century. It is mentioned four centuries later in the travelogue of

Benjamin of Tudela. To this day Schechter's discoveries haven't been exhaustively studied, but the Cairo *genizah* material has been the subject of rigorous scholarly work by Shlomo Dov Goitein, who produced a six-volume portrayal of life in the Middle Ages, a magnificent view of the overlapping intellectual and everyday spheres in the Judeo-Islamic world.

VA: Where are the texts from the Ben Ezra *genizah* housed today?

IS: They are divided between Cambridge University and The Jewish Theological Seminary in New York City.

VA: Like the Torah, the Qur'an cannot simply be discarded.

IS: Think of the tunnels filled with thousands upon thousands of Qur'ans beneath Chiltan Mountain, in the Quetta heights of Pakistan's Baluchistan province. Think of the magisterial cemetery of books discovered in 1972 at the Great Mosque at San'a, in Yemen. How many undisclosed depositories such as these await their Columbus? Not too long ago, there was an international controversy ignited by a *Newsweek* reportage that claimed American soldiers had flushed copies of the Qur'an down the toilet. This brings me back to my comments on the essay "The First Book." Why is the image of the Qur'an in such a context incendiary? I doubt the same reaction would take place if a photograph were released in which someone— say an Afghani, a Peruvian, or a Briton—were caught peeing on a copy of Dostoyevsky's *Crime and Punishment.*

Literature can be destroyed, but it cannot be desecrated. In prophetic religions, the sacred text is at once reservoir and conduit of heavenly information. To dispose of it in prosaic ways is to violate the rules that distinguish the pure from the impure.

VA: What do Christians do with old Bibles?

IS: Although to my knowledge there isn't a prohibition against discarding them, people just don't do it. Even though to a Christian the artifact is just paper, glue, and ink, there is an important attachment to it. The book itself isn't holy, it is its content, its message that is. One reason for not wanting to discard old bibles might be that Christians often write on the page, stressing a word, underlining a sentence, and highlighting a passage. It might be due to the fact that a particular copy has been a close companion in one's spiritual journey. My own view is that, unlike Jews, Muslims, and Hindus, Christians have a different connection to language. Churches don't read Scripture in Hebrew, Aramaic, or Greek. And though the pope may still celebrate Mass in Latin, almost everyone else does it in the vernacular. This is because the medium isn't the message. Indeed, the Christian tradition of biblical translation stresses the fact that the Scriptures need to be understood by the masses.

VA: Are *genizot* libraries?

IS: Only metaphorically. The library is a house of knowledge. Our modern libraries are quite sanitized. Books are meticulously catalogued, at least in modern times. They circulate under a specific regime. The temperature inside is controlled. There are desks, magazines, computers, etc. One cannot talk out loud in them. But libraries have not been thus always. Often when I go into one I feel I'm entering another realm. Is this good? I'm not sure. These days libraries are like museums: a marketplace of artifacts designed to impress you but not necessarily to make you think. Houses of knowledge are houses of study. Why then speak quietly? Why not debate others in intellectual explorations? I suggest institutionalizing at least one day when "users"—I dislike the term—are allowed to scream and shout in a library about anything they find in a book.

VA: Are book cemeteries found only in the Judeo-Islamic tradition?

IS: They are found elsewhere, too. In the Buddhist kingdom of Ganhara, in eastern Afghanistan, a container was found with some twenty-nine scrolls in Kharoshti script. They date back two millennia. The fragments had been put away near a monastery according to the proper burial rituals. In addition, in 1973 a British archeologist found in north Northumberland a Roman fort called Vindolanda. From its pits he unearthed some fifteen hundred texts, among them Carthaginian letters and official documents.

VA: Are there modern book cemeteries?

IS: Time capsules became fashionable in the late twentieth century. NASA designed a couple. The city of Atlanta built a chamber that houses 640,000 odd pages from eight hundred "classics in the arts and sciences" reproduced in microfilm and sealed in nitrogen gas for preservation. And then there's Oglethorpe University's converted indoor swimming pool known as the Crypt of Civilization completed in 1940 that houses an assortment of artifacts, not just books. That chamber is supposed to remain sealed until 8,113, a date the president of the institution and the mastermind of the project, Dr. Thornwell Jacobs, came up with after bizarre calculations based on the first Egyptian calendar. Book cemeteries often become even more fanciful. *The New York Times*, for example, hired the world-renowned Spanish architect, Santiago Calatrava, to design a massive enclosure, dubbed the Times Capsule, to be opened in the year 3000. It contains a millennium-worth of materials. There are about 10,000 similar capsules throughout the United States. How many of these are likely to be found by the citizens of tomorrow?

VA: Is the cemetery another emblematic metaphor for the library?

IS: How so?

VA: One frequently hears about the death of literature.

IS: In the last few years, I've taken to regularly visit cemeteries in the areas where I've lived: Mexico City, Jerusalem, Amherst, and Wellfleet, Massachusetts. These are quiet, meditative spaces. Popular culture infuses an element of spookiness to them. But they aren't frightening. Instead, I find them appeasing. I carefully study the tombstones, the graphics engraved in them (some even have photographs), the stones and flowers and flags people pay tribute with, the areas designed for "recreation." Yes, I read myself into the place as well. I imagine the lives led by each of those buried in the cemetery, their connection with others buried in the place. Francisco de Quevedo, the sixteenth-century Spanish poet, has an astonishing sonnet, known as *Soneto* 131, about books, in which he connects death and wisdom: Translating Quevedo's poetry into English is a thankless task. (His dreams, novels and *discursos* are different.) The versions I've come across sound as if done by a teenager on drugs. Perhaps that might explain why he's almost unknown by those who do not speak Spanish, in spite of his astonishing powers. Surprisingly, Sor Juana Inés de La Cruz has traveled well across linguistic lines. And there are workmanlike renditions of the poetry of Jorge Manrique, Fray Luis de León, Lope de Vega, and San Juan de la Cruz. But not of Quevedo's (and, of course, absolutely not of Luis de Gongora's). In any case, this poem was composed in a finca called Torre de Juan Abad:

> Retirado en la paz de estos desiertos,
> con pocos, pero doctos libros juntos,
> vivo en conversación con los difuntos
> y escucho con mis ojos a los muertos.
>
> Si no siempre entendidos, siempre abiertos,
> o enmiendan, o fecundan mis asuntos;
> y en músicos callados contrapuntos
> al sueño de la vida hablan despiertos.

Las grandes almas que la muerte ausenta,
de injurias de los años, vengadora,
libra, ¡oh gran don Iosef!, docta la emprenta.

En fuga irrevocable huye la hora;
pero aquélla el mejor cálculo cuenta
que en la lección y estudios nos mejora.

CHAPTER EIGHT

Censorship

Wherever they burn books they will also, in the end, burn human beings.

—Heinrich Heine

Verónica Albin: What is censorship?

Ilan Stavans: To deliberately expurgate material for specific reasons. Ironically, the *OED* lists divergent definitions for the word "censor," one historical, the other consuetudinary: "the title of two magistrates in ancient Rome, who drew up the register or census of the citizens, etc., and had the supervision of public morals"; and "one who exercises official or officious supervision over morals and conduct."

VA: An ancient practice...

IS: Although one easily misunderstood. The First Amendment to the U.S. Constitution states: "Congress shall make no law respecting an establishment of religion, or prohibiting the free exercise thereof, or abridging the freedom of speech or of the press, or the right of the people peacefully to assemble and to petition the Government for a redress of grievances." In the democratic world, this maxim has become a touchstone, one that not every society is able to handle. Voltaire once famously said: "I disagree with everything you say—but will fight to the death for your right to say it." Not to allow others to disagree, to be intolerant of opinions different from ours, constitutes censorship. On the other hand, the late U.S. Supreme Court chief justice Oliver Wendell Holmes stated: "Freedom of speech does not include the liberty to shout FIRE! in a crowded theater." In other words, words have echoes: they carry consequences. And people are responsible for those consequences. Not to be allowed to cry FIRE! in a crowded theater, is that censorship? Not quite, although it does impose limitations on freedom.

Censorship is the cry wolf of modern political debates. The liberal world wants people to believe that censorship is extant where tyranny prevails. This sentiment is traceable to the Enlightenment, which fought for individual freedom. Voltaire, Diderot, and, in general, the French Encyclopedists fought against the obscurantism of medieval times. Their quest was for equality, justice, and freedom for all. But the dreams of the Enlightenment in France, England, Germany, and the United States were never fully realized. Censorship is a feature of every hierarchy—be it capitalist, communist, democratic, etc.—where a few are in control of the information. So the question never is "Is there censorship here?" but "What kind of censorship is to be found here?"

VA: And there is also self-censorship.

IS: No act of human communication is ever, in any way, free of some degree of control, restriction, and even, yes, the suppression of information. In our daily interactions— with friends and family, for instance—we ponder the consequences of our words. An average stream of consciousness might be: "If I say 'I love you,' will she reciprocate? Maybe she won't, not so soon at least. After all, we've only seen each other a couple of times." This type of self-imposed limitation is, somehow, a form of self-censorship. Each of us is born with an inherent mechanism that calibrates our interaction with society.

VA: I sense a pessimistic tone in your statement.

IS: I read somewhere that the difference between an optimist and a pessimist is that the optimist hopes ours is the best of all possible universes while the pessimist knows it is.

VA: What are the earliest most visible examples of censorship?

IS: Again, the discussion of censorship is a by-product of the Enlightenment. The French Revolution gave us the vocabulary. Once we made it our own, of course, it is possible to look back in time and find benchmarks in the history of censorship that make this a practice as old as humankind. The Bible has a plethora of cases. Cain misinforms God about Abel's true fate. The news about Joseph's fate reaches Jacob in oblique fashion. In Greece, Socrates is the ultimate martyr to censorship. Indeed, it strikes me as ironic that this most open-minded of philosophers is remembered not through his own words, but through those of his authoritarian student Plato. Isn't that a perverse historical twist? In the Far East, the examples are copious. Emperor Shih Huang Ti of China is known for his barbaric colonial enterprises. He ordered the building of the Great Wall of China, which would protect his people from invading armies. But in the year 213 BCE, through his first minister Li Si, he also ordered the destruction of every single book in the kingdom—except those on medicine, agriculture, pharmacy, and fortune-telling. These parallel efforts have struck many as diabolic: geographically, Shih Huang Ti closed his domain to outside influences; chronologically, he sought to start the paths of history with himself. Not casually, the emperor thought of his person as "the first, the auspicious, the godlike." Sigmund Freud once suggested that proof of human progress is that books and not people are burnt at the stake today. His view is disingenuous, of course. True, the autos-da-fé by the Holy Office of the Inquisition in Seville in the fifteenth century are no longer in store. But exile, imprisonment, torture, and death of dissidents is a common practice around the world. As for the burning of books, if that is a thermometer of the cultural malaise, the patient's illness is as threatening as it has always been. Books were burnt in the Hellenistic period and they still are in the present, from *Krystallnacht* to Kansas City in 1996. When it isn't burning per se, it is simply banning. Think of Joyce's *Ulysses*, Nabokov's *Lolita*, D.H. Lawrence's *Lady Chatterley's Lover*, Henry Miller's *Tropic of Cancer,* and *Harry Potter*...the list is long, and, unfortunately, still being updated today. And if it isn't books, it is other artifacts: songs, plays, movies, videos, DVDs. Or else, it is people themselves. To die for one's ideals is the ultimate sacrifice, of course. What censors never understand is that people might be killed but not ideals.

VA: What kind of person accepts the job of censor?

IS: The Russians have a delightful word: "apparatchik." It isn't quite a bureaucrat, nor is it a self-loathing individual. Some would argue, of course, that under certain circumstances everyone is capable of becoming a censor. I thoroughly disagree. This, in my mind, is a type of personality easily compelled to be a sell-out, to become mediocre. Eduardo Galeano has a memorable paragraph on the chain reaction I would describe as "the art of acquiescence" in modern society. It is part of an essay called "Cemetery of Words." It reads:

> The system that programmes the computer that alarms the banker who alerts the ambassador who dines with the general who summons the president who informs the minister who threatens the managing director who humiliates the manager who shouts at the boss who harasses the white-collar worker who despises the manual worker who ill-treats his wife who hits the child who kicks the dog.

This is what mediocrity is about: to hide behind someone else's actions.

VA: Translators are also said to "hide behind someone else's actions."

IS: Translators and censors no doubt have elements in common. And they have also shared objectives, I hasten to say. I don't say this with any animosity. On the contrary, it could be said that I'm obsessed with the art of translation. In the scale of intellectual endeavors, translators have my highest esteem. Still, translators have been used by tyrannical regimes to quietly expurgate works of material considered indecent or subversive by those in power. Yes, in the troubled history of human sins, translators are not automatically exonerated. They belong in Dante's Ninth Circle of Hell, reserved for sinners of malice and inconsistency.

VA: I shall return to that topic shortly. But first, one often connects censorship with the intransigence of fanaticism.

IS: To fanatical regimes and institutions, I would say, that religion often plays a lead role in the shaping of the intransigent mentality. The act of consolidating a faith involves defining others as heretical. In that sense, St. Paul is among the earliest censors in the history of Western Civilization. The Roman Catholic *Indexes* of the sixteenth and later centuries were justified by Paul's initiation of clerical bowdlerization. There are hundreds of illustrated covers displaying Pauline converts destroying books. The long papal succession is the one in charge of making the Catholic Church coalesce as an institution by refuting and antagonizing others. Gregory IX, for instance, was the first Catholic leader to officially forbid the Talmud, describing it as a piece of Jewish propaganda. Keep in mind that the Babylonian and Palestinian versions were only available in the original Aramaic. In other words, censorship doesn't imply direct access to the banned source. It is enough to typecast it as dangerous to seek its elimination.

VA: Whenever I read the titles in the Indexes of forbidden books issued by the Catholic Church, I can't help but smile. The first Spanish one is called *Index librorum qui prohibendur* (Valdés, 1559) but soon enough the censors start competing with "new and improved" products and go from the simple index to *Novus Index librorum prohibitorum et expurgatorum* (Zapata, 1632) to *Novissimus librorum prohibitorum et expurgatorum Index* (Sotomayor, 1640). I do not smile, however, when I read their contents.

IS: The *Indexes* gave access to unauthorized titles. They also listed burnable books. It always astonishes me how punctilious censors are. It is never enough to seek the eradication of the forbidden fruit. Equally, if not more, important is the detailed description of it, and what makes it so undesirable. They often sought the prohibition of a book from mass consumption, which doesn't mean that the educated elite—or at least the censors themselves—couldn't read them.

VA: This brings to mind the secret libraries available without restriction to the elite and the censors such as *L'Enfer*, modeled on a purported similar library in the Vatican, and that of the British Museum: the Private Case collection.

IS: Yes, *L'Enfer*, literally "The Hell," established in 1791, is the collection of obscene, suppressed, and otherwise forbidden books held by the Bibliothèque Nationale in

Paris. The collection was in a shambles and lost many volumes to pilfering until it was catalogued by Guillaume Apollinaire in 1913. It is estimated to contain around four thousand volumes. The Private Case collection, housed originally in the British Museum, in Bloomsbury, London, at one time was said to number twenty thousand tomes, although theft, vandalism, and other causes have reduced it to somewhere between eighteen hundred and five thousand erotic, indecent, obscene, and pornographic volumes, depending on who's counting. It includes material published over more than three centuries in England, France, Spain, Portugal, Italy, Germany, the Low Countries... and it even includes works in Latin. The Private Case holdings surpass, both in quality and scope, similar "restricted" collections such as The Hell, those of the Library of Congress in Washington, and the Bodleian at Oxford and, yes, some say it even bests the Vatican's own very vast holdings on erotica, blasphemy, and freemasonry, among other risqué topics. This said, it should be mentioned that the Dominican priest, Father Leonard Boyle O.P., retired Prefect (chief librarian) of the Vatican Apostolic Library denied to his death in 1999 that the Vatican has ever held such a collection. In addition, Gershon Legman, a prominent student of erotica who helped compile a bibliography of porn for Alfred Kinsey, has stated that the Vatican doesn't have any really erotic books, claiming that the raciest are some fairly tame volumes from the classical era such as a copy of Ovid's *Ars Amatoria* filled with Latin poetry, and Aristophanes'

Lysistrata. The Vatican Library is rarely opened to scholars, and the few that are permitted to cross its threshold are carefully screened, monitored, and given restricted access to very specific materials, so we might never know what its stacks really hold under lock and key. But as for the two other large European erotica holdings, while *L'Enfer* remains closed to this day to all but researchers with special permits, in 1963 it was announced that the Private Case, with its pressmarks "P.C." and "Cup." (for the "Cupboard")—up to this point available only to library staff and those with contacts in high places—would be gradually transferred into the General Catalog. By 1965 this was done, although, from what I know, the readers of books pressmarked "P.C." and "Cup." are still required to sit at a special table in the library.

VA: You mentioned the prohibition against the Talmud. Why was Judaism such a threat to the Catholic Church?

IS: St. Augustine is clear on this matter. The sheer existence of Jews is proof of the passion of Jesus Christ. Jews should be vilified, even attacked, but never killed, for this would deprive future generations of the proof itself. The controversy on *la limpieza de sangre*, purity of blood, in Spain from the fifteenth to the sixteenth centuries, emphasized lineage as proof of authenticity. What wasn't pure wasn't authentic. Those outside the realm were considered undesirable, their intellectual contribution questioned. The journey of thinkers and poets in medieval Spain who descended from Jewish families, such as Santa Teresa de Jesús, Juan Luis Vives, Gil Vicente, and Fray Luis de León, to name but a few, is replete with censoring episodes. But people with less "suspicious" ancestry are also emblematic. Take the case of the Salamanca grammarian Antonio de Nebrija who was free from the Jewish stigma but was nonetheless censored by virtue of being an intellectual.

VA: You discuss him frequently in your work from *Spanglish: The Making of a New American Language* to *Dictionary Days*.

IS: In 1470, having spent a decade studying in Bologna, Nebrija returned to Spain, and, while teaching at Salamanca from 1473 to 1486, he wrote a series of fifty commentaries on the Holy Scripts. Rumors of apostasy began to circulate. Diego de Deza, bishop of Palencia and Salamanca and still Grand Inquisitor, became concerned. Maybe that is why Nebrija abandoned his teaching post and embarked on the study of lexicography, for which, of course, he became known posthumously. Still, in 1505 he finished his commentaries, at which time Deza, by now an archbishop, had the manuscript confiscated. This is a portion of a letter from Nebrija to Cardinal Cisneros. It is an extraordinary plea for intellectual freedom. He describes Spain as a country suffocated by mediocrity:

> Me llaman temerario porque con sólo el arte de Gramática me meto por las demás artes y disciplinas no como tránsfuga, sino como explorador y centinela para ver lo que hace cada uno con su profesión. Lo que hice antes con la medicina y con el derecho civil, eso mismo quiero hacer ahora con las letras sagradas, protestando que no saldré fuera de mi jurisdicción.

They say I'm rash because availing myself only of the
Grammarian's art I venture into other arts and disciplines,
not as a rogue, but rather as an explorer and sentry to see
what each one is doing in his own profession. What I did
before with medicine and civil law, I wish to do as well with
sacred texts, and I shall do so with the promise of never
infringing upon the borders of my domain.

The tone reminds me of Sor Juana Inés de la Cruz's
brave "Response to Sor Filotea," another lucid manifesto
against ecclesiastical censorship. In the same epistle,
which is quoted in J. Olmedo's Nebrija, *develador de la
barbarie*, Nebrija adds:

> ¿Qué si no será el mío que no sé pensar sino cosas difíciles,
> ni acometer sino arduas, ni publicar sino las que me dan
> más disgustos? Si me acomodara a la actitud de mis amigos
> y empleara mis vigilias en las fábulas y ficciones de los
> poetas, si me dedicara a escribir historias y, como dice el
> poeta, todo lo viera de color de rosas, me querrían bien,
> me alabarían, me darían mil parabienes. Pero como inves-
> tigo en la tierra aquellas cosas cuyo conocimiento persevera
> en el cielo, me llaman temerario, sacrílego y falsario, y no
> falta nada para que me hagan comparecer ante los jueces
> cargado de cadenas... ¿Qué hacer en un país donde se pre-
> mia a los que corrompen las Sagradas Letras y, al contrario,
> los que corrigen lo defectuoso, restituyen lo falsificado y
> enmiendan lo falso y erróneo, se ven infamados y anatem-
> izados y aun condenados a muerte indigna si tratan de
> defender su manera de pensar? [...] ¿He de decir a la fuerza
> que no sé lo que sé? ¿Qué esclavitud o qué poder es éste
> tan despótico? ¿Qué digo decir? Ni escribirlo encerrado

entre cuatro paredes, ni murmurarlo en voz baja en un agujero de la pared, ni pensarlo a solas te permiten.

It is but my lot in life to be incapable of thinking except of difficult things, nor do but difficult ones, nor publish except those that are most aggravating? If I were to conform to my friends' attitude and spent my late-night vigils immersed in fables or in the imaginings of poets, If I were to devote myself to writing stories, and, as the poet says, see everything through a rose-colored glass, they would like me well enough, they would praise me, they would congratulate me a thousand times. But since on this Earth I investigate those things known only in Heaven, they say I'm rash, sacrilegious, and mendacious and it would take but little else to make me appear before the judges weighted down with chains... What is one to do in a country where those who corrupt the Holy Texts get rewarded and those, those who mend what is flawed, restore truth to the falsehoods and amend what is false and what is wrong are defamed and anathematized and even condemned to ignominious death if they attempt to defend their ideas? [...] Must I be forced to say that I do not know what I know? What slavery or what power is this one so tyrannical? What is there to say? Writing down one's thoughts confined by four walls, whispering them to a hole in the wall, or thinking about them inside one's head, even that they forbid.

Cardinal Cisneros eventually sided with Nebrija, to whom he awarded a job in Alcalá de Henares.

VA: The same zealotry one finds in the Catholic Church is traceable to totalitarian regimes. This is because a dictatorship only accepts a single version of the truth. Everything else is anathema.

IS: There is Fidel Castro's famous sentence: "*O con la revolución, o en su contra,*" either you're with the revolution, or you're against it. Needless to say, it is, in spirit, the same Manichaean line delivered to foreign governments by George W. Bush shortly after 9/11: "either you're with us, or you're with the terrorists." George Lucas inserted a version of it in the third installment of the *Star Wars* saga: *Revenge of the Sith*. One of the most celebrated dissidents in Castro's Cuba was the poet Heberto Padilla. I'm fond of one of his poems, entitled "Instructions on how to enter a new society," where he recommends: "One: be an optimist" and "Two: be discreet, correct, obedient."

Padilla, you might remember, was at the heart of an intellectual scandal, the so-called Padilla Affair. Just like the protagonist of Arthur Koestler's anti-tyranny novel *Darkness at Noon*, he was forced to publicly confess to crimes he might not have committed. This prompted an international uproar that made Jean-Paul Sartre, Alberto Moravia, Octavio Paz, and Susan Sontag, among others, break with the Cuban Revolution. Ironically, his poem is as accurate a description of life under Communism as it is in a Capitalist society.

I want to return to the topic of translation. It is often the case that translators living in restrictive environments, such as Franco's Spain and Hitler's Germany, work with texts originated in less restrictive settings and have to conform to authority. However, translators have also been known to subvert the status quo while working within a restrictive environment in an effort to be read unequivocally in a less restrictive one. In *"La traduction des textes déjà censurés,"* Teresa Tomaszkiewicz explains that Pope Jean Paul II self-censored the homilies he prepared for his first visit to then communist Poland. Polish translators working with foreign journalists wished to give nonnative speakers full access to the meaning of the Pope's multilayered, and subversive, source language texts understood fully only by Polish speakers.

Yet censorship is alive and well in America. When Michael Moore was seeking a distributor in the United States for his documentary *Fahrenheit 9/11*, Republicans looked for ways to make its journey to the local theaters an impossible one. Likewise, conservative pundits regularly complain that the liberal media doesn't allow room for their opinions. This debate about censorship takes place under the watchful eye of Congress, the Senate, and the U.S. Supreme Court.

VA: In the essay "Ink, Inc.," included in *Dictionary Days*, you talk about another censoring force: the corporate environment.

IS: That, to me, is by far the most noxious. Enter a Barnes & Noble anywhere in America and what do you find? An overabundance of books. The staff hardly knows what's in stock. The so-called hot items are shoved down people's throats while more refined books are hidden from view. And when these books are showcased—say *Wuthering Heights*, *The Bridge of San Luis Rey*, and *Pride and Prejudice*—they are marketed as disposable items. A trip to my local mega-store usually drives me out of my mind.

VA: There is also the complaint that foreign literature doesn't find its way to American readers.

IS: It surely doesn't. Publishers often excuse themselves by saying that the United States is an insular nation, one allergic to outside forces. There is truth to this but it doesn't justify the trepidation in investing in non-English-speaking authors. Germany and Israel are models in this respect— the number of books translated in these countries is astonishingly high. For instance, how many books in Arabic were translated into English by New York publishers in 2004? Three.

VA: Should the dearth of foreign novels released in English translation by publishers in the United States be considered a form of censorship?

IS: Absolutely. And an endorsement of parochialism, too. New York publishers excuse themselves by saying that such books don't sell. Is it because Americans aren't interested in what goes on in the rest of the world? Maybe. But isn't the curse of an empire to decline and fall as a result of its narcissism? Either way, the lack of foreign novels available constitutes an endorsement of collective blindness.

VA: How about Spain?

IS: It fares better than the United States. Ironically, authors from other Spanish-speaking countries, from Argentina to Peru, from Colombia to Mexico, regularly complain that their books aren't available in the Iberian Peninsula.

So is the colonial structure still in place? By the way, the worst record in terms of censorship-cum-publishing in the Americas is held by Cuba.

VA: It's understandable.

IS: And regrettable, too.

VA: On the issue of Cuba, the translator Esther Allen, in an essay called "Doors, Windows and the Office of Foreign Assets Control," says that when she embarked on the translation of Alejo Carpentier's only work that remained untranslated into English, the brief piece "*La ciudad de las columnas,*" she didn't realize she was embarking on an illegal activity, since Cuba is an embargoed country.

IS: Similarly, when I edited *The Oxford Book of Latin American Essays*, I commissioned a translation of a piece about Josephine Baker in Cuba by Nicolás Guillén. When time came to request permission from the Cuban government agency responsible for such projects, the ordeal I went through was nothing short of Kafkaesque. They required an exorbitant amount of money and wanted a difficult-to-comply contract. That's what ends up happening when literature is left to the state to handle: a sorrowful act.

On the subject of translation and censorship, one should recognize that, at heart, they are moved by the same rationale—to make pertinent material available to readers in a fashion suitable to the taste of an individual or elite. Both are gatekeepers who stand at key control points and rule over what gets in and what stays out of any given cultural or linguistic territory. Obviously, there are innumerable cases of translators whose job it becomes to restrict and suppress information. All cases are ideologically charged. Think of the translations into various European tongues of the *Nights*, also known as *The Book of the Thousand and One Nights* as well as *The Thousand Nights and One Night*. It is universally acknowledged that the rather pedestrian original is filled with flying carpets, marvels, and talismans. The English, French, German, and even Spanish versions, done predominantly in the nineteenth century and early parts of the twentieth, infused the text with a stylistic sophistication unrecognizable to the original Arabic, Farsi, or Hindi readers. But the transgressions go farther. Captain Richard Francis Burton and Edward Lane inserted episodes of their own invention in the English editions—from the ones on Aladdin to those of Abu al-Hassan and the forty thieves. Their Victorian prudishness also made them eliminate what they believed to be sexually explicit fragments. Similar devices were implemented by Galland in French and Littman in German. Obviously, it wasn't carelessness what prompted them to act. It was overzealousness. The *Arabian Nights* is only one example in a long history of egregious abuses by translators.

VA: How about cases of so-called permitted dissent?

IS: Every totalitarian system incorporates forms of self-immolation. The Catholic Church invites people to repent through confession, Mao Zedong encouraged children during the Cultural Revolution to denounce "non-revolutionary behavior," fascism forced people to sacrifice their needs in favor of a nationalistic ideal. Yet these systems behave according to cycles. At times they allow for some openness and elasticity only to retrench to more rigid mores. Dissent is at times encouraged, then curtailed. The reason has to do with internal tension: total subjugation is impossible, just as complete freedom is unattainable. In Cuba in the eighteenth century, once a year—on the occasion of a carnival—black slaves were allowed to curse the Spanish rulers and even throw eggs and tomatoes at government buildings while their owners were conveniently on vacation. Psychologically, the value of such release of frustration is incommensurable.

VA: You've written a powerful essay on the role of translation during the conquest of the Americas. It was collected in your book *The Essential Ilan Stavans*. In the context of colonization, how are native translators linked to the power structures?

IS: During the conquest of the Mexico and Peru translators played a major role. They served as conduits between the two clashing civilizations. The myth of La Malinche also portrays some of them as traitors. As you know, Doña Marina, as she is known in Spanish, became Hernán Cortés's interpreter and mistress. Sex, power, and words...

VA: Talking about La Malinche, I want to pursue, albeit briefly, the issue of gender. In 1603, John Florio, the English translator of Montaigne, inexorably linked translation and the status of women by claiming that since translations are always flawed, they were well suited to be done by females. What can you tell us about the female presence in literary translation?

IS: There are exemplary cases of female translators. In the English language realm, think, for instance, of Mary Herbert (1561–1621), translator of Petrarch's *Triumph of Death* and Philip Sidney's sister; Jane Lumley (1537–1576), translator of Euripides's *Iphigenia*; and Margaret More Roper (1505–1544), daughter of Sir Thomas More and translator of Erasmus of Rotterdam's *Precatio Dominica*. Erasmus considered her the "ornament of Britain." Anne Bacon (?–1610), mother of Francis Bacon, was a translator too. The list is emphatically shorter than the one devoted to male translators, simply because the humanities from the Hellenistic period until the early half of the twentieth century were the territory of males.

VA: I wonder if censorship in a multilingual nation where several tongues are used (India and Luxemburg, for instance) is different than one in a monolingual one (say Poland and Hungary).

IS: My instinct is to say that polyglotism allows for more openness.

VA: You mentioned *Lady Chatterley's Lover*. When the novel went on trial, Lawrence argued that to return to Chaucer is to return to innocence, that time before the fall where the excremental taboo had not yet sullied the mind; a return to those times before taboos on the representation of sex, where things could be called by their true names. Is *Lady Chatterley's Lover* an innocent novel?

IS: There are no innocent novels. Innocence is not an attribute of the novel as a literary genre. Indeed, I believe the novel is about the end of innocence.

VA: But conservative thinkers, taking the role of *custos morum*, argue that censorship is necessary to protect our children's innocence.

IS: How does one protect someone's innocence—by blinding them to what surrounds them? Children are not innocent, they are extremely curious and inquisitive, and find their way in the world. It is our duty as adults to grant the necessary tools for them to understand that world as best as possible.

VA: On the dangers of fiction, in March 2005, the Archbishop of Genoa, Tarcisio Cardinal Bertone, who until four years ago was a member of the Congregation for the Doctrine of the Faith, broke the Vatican's silence on *The Da Vinci Code*. He told Vatican Radio that no one should read it and Catholic bookstores should stop selling it. And in remarks to *Il Giornale*, a conservative newspaper, Bertone stated that the book "aims to discredit the Church and its history through gross and absurd manipulations." Cardinal Bertone's chief worry, as stated, was that "there is a very real risk that many people who read it will believe that the fables it contains are true." What do you make of Bertone's comments about the nature of fiction?

IS: Fiction is, by definition, a lie. As a society, we pay novelists to lie for us, that is, to build engaging plots out of the stuff of dreams. Why is fiction the favorite genre of the bourgeoisie? The answer is easy: it's a class infatuated with its own dreams. The statement by Cardinal Bertone isn't without precedent, though. In colonial Latin America, up until late in the nineteenth century, novels were forbidden from circulation. The crime? Potentially inciting the masses to entertain unacceptable ideas. Fiction has always been understood to have a double edge—it allows for an escape from routine and it also showcases the possibilities of freedom.

VA: You also talked briefly about pornography. What is the difference between pornography and obscenity?

IS: The *OED* refuses to define the word "obscenity." Instead, it offers the following synonyms: impurity, indecency, lewdness (especially of language). "Pornography," on the other hand, is described—prudishly—as the "description of the life, manners, etc., of prostitutes and their patrons; hence, the expression or suggestion of obscene or unchaste subjects in literature or art." I'm struck by the social changes experienced from the time, in the early nineteenth century, when the Oxford dons compiled this definition, to the present. Nowadays pornography is hardly limited to the realm of pimps and whores. Actually, the word has become politically charged—a taboo of sorts. Is pornography beyond freedom of speech? Can one not scream FIRE! in a crowded theater but accuse others of lewd behavior? Has tolerance gone too far allowing a type of sexual explicitness that is offensive? The mantra of the marketplace, of course, is simple: if it sells, it ought to be manufactured.

VA: In 1853, in Manheim, Germany, the statue of the *Venus de Milo* was tried in court for her nudity—and was convicted and condemned. Almost a hundred years later, in December of 1952, the Cyprus Tourist Office used the figure on posters it sent to Kuwait, hoping to attract Arab tourists. Sheik Abdullah al Salim al Sebah banned them. It wasn't the nudity that was problematic, it seems, for it offended no one. The problem was the lack of arms on the fair maiden. Under Islamic law, recidivist thieves have their hands cut off, and the Kuwaitis, seeing the armless statue—Sheik Abdullah surmised—might assume that all Cypriot girls were hardened criminals.

IS: A lovely example of counter-censorship. But I want to offer you another one. A while ago I referred to the Talmud. How does the compiler of the Talmud deal with apostasy? Through silence. One of the most intriguing cases of heresy in rabbinical Judaism is that of Elisha ben Avuyah, who lived in Palestine approximately between 70 and 135 CE. Ben Avuyah was a friend of Rabbi Akiva. What was his sin? He was obsessed with Greek philosophy, eventually losing his faith in the Almighty. The Talmud includes only a minimal amount of information about him. In the rare occasions where he is mentioned, he is described as an *Acher*: the other. Silence, needless to say, is also what publishers and translators embrace when facing a difficult challenge.

VA: Similarly, during the nearly four decades that Spain was ruled by General Francisco Franco—from 1936 to 1975—cultural manifestations were closely monitored and controlled by the Fascist military authority as well as by the Church. A salient characteristic of this span of time is that it was long enough to allow for the creation of new ways of receiving imported texts, and, more important, for the manipulation in a certain direction of the publishing industry in the Iberian Peninsula, favoring certain authors and certain types of literary production over others.

IS: The strategy was to divert attention by translating works that were ideologically "clean," whose plots and settings were both mentally and physically distant, for example, far-West novels, spy novels, sci-fi stories, etc. It's an old technique: Keep the populace in a state of somnolence by feeding it only with what's irrelevant. Sports, for instance.

VA: In April 2005, Representative Gerald Allen, a Republican from Alabama, drafted a bill that would have barred any gay writers and playwrights—and books or plays with homosexual characters—from Alabama public schools and libraries, and state-funded universities. Which banned books, plays, or authors under the Allen bill would you consider going to war for, Ilan?

IS: Representative Allen forgets the allure of the forbidden. We're curious about what we can't get. My prediction is that gay literature will become immensely popular in Alabama as a result of his foolish effort. In any case, war isn't the solution. My response would be to challenge his bill under the premise of First Amendment rights.

VA: When he was England's Poet Laureate, John Dryden said in his preface to his version of the *Aeneid*. "I have endeavoured to make Virgil speak such English as he would himself have spoken, if he had been born in England, and in this present Age." In Lawrence Venuti's words: "A skeptic might well wonder why Virgil should come back as Dryden instead of an epic poet who lived in the same period and wrote his epic without rhyme: John Milton. Should we not expect an English Virgil to be more attracted to the grand style of *Paradise Lost*?"

IS: I have almost twenty different translations of *Don Quixote* into Shakespeare's tongue, from the earliest one published when the second part of Cervantes's masterpiece, released in 1615, had not yet appeared, to the most recent by Edith Grossman, published in 2003. The various translators have taken the liberty of adapting the adventures of the Knight of the Sorrowful Countenance and his loyal servant as they see fit. They've eliminated segments and expanded others. Equally important has been the effort to "update" the Spanish of the early parts of the seventeenth century to whatever period the translator deems appropriate. And so, Grossman, for instance, doesn't take the contemporary reader back to Cervantes's time. That would make her effort unappealing. Since in her view Cervantes wrote with ease and accessibility in 1605, her strategy has been to make her *Quixote* easy and accessible today by using an average lexicon. Should we not expect an English knight to be more attracted to the so-called Golden Age of Spain in the period of the defeat of the Invincible Armada, just like we would expect an English Virgil to be more suitable to the grand style of

Paradise Lost? The response is yes and no. It all depends on what the translator seeks to achieve. Does he want us to travel back to the author's time or does he instead want for the author to travel to the present day? Interestingly, I just finished editing a volume for Penguin Classics called *Rubén Darío: Selected Writings*. It is the most comprehensive anthology of the Nicaraguan poet's oeuvre in English. The section of poetry was translated by Greg Simon and Steven White, and they chose to bring Darío's poetry to the present. The prose, on the other hand, was translated by Andrew Hurley. He used somewhat stilted end-of-the-nineteenth-century English to recreate Darío's symbolist, Parnassian manner. In other words, the two devices are offered in the same book.

VA: In *"Desfontaines travesti,"* Benoit Léger examines the first French importation through translation—and rewriting—of the Henry Fielding novel, *The History of the Adventures of Joseph Andrews*, published in 1743. The translation was done by Pierre-François Guyot Desfontaines at a time in France when this genre was not considered high literature. What the French translator did was adopt the persona of *"Une Dame angloise,"* which allowed him, through his paratext, to kill two birds with one stone: criticize Fielding's novel as well as the mores of his French contemporaries.

IS: The translator as author—ah, what a delicious conundrum! It makes me think of Borges's labyrinthine relationship with Norman Thomas Di Giovanni, an American translator of Italian descent. Di Giovanni met and befriended the Argentine in Cambridge, Massachusetts. In order to bring out Borges's work in English (he signed a multi-book contract with the publisher E.P. Dutton for Borges's stories, poems, and essays), the agreement was that Di Giovanni would move to Buenos Aires. But his impartiality as translator was soon replaced by a "hands-on" activist approach. He asked the Argentine to accept an added and/or twisted sentence in the translation, then asked Borges to change the original Spanish text in a subsequent reprint in order to reflect the change made. An ugly picture! Indeed, Di Giovanni was known to have the upper hand in their friendship. This lasted until, or so lore has it, Borges was having dinner with friends when the phone rang; it was Di Giovanni. Aware of the tyranny, Borges's friends had for some time encouraged him to terminate the liaison. He finally found the guts to do it that day. He picked up the receiver, briefly told the translator this was to be their last conversation, then put the phone down. He never spoke to Di Giovanni again.

"Une Dame angloise" also brings to mind *Les belles infidèles*—a delightful term, don't you think? Jean Delisle offers the following quote in *Translators Through History*:

> The Académie was established in 1635 by King Louis XIII at the instigation of Cardinal Richelieu (1585–1642), but this institutionalization itself was an attempt to exert some control over the group of literati that had begun to meet in the house of Valentin Conrart. During the Académie's first years, Conrart was the originator of many works

of translation produced by individuals and groups. He gave instructions and advice. From Conrart's circle arose the man whose new way of translating was to become characteristic of his time—Nicolas Perrot d'Ablancourt (1606–64), who was elected to the Académie in 1637. The term "belle infidèle" was coined to describe his translation of Lucian's *True History*. In his prefaces, Perrot d'Ablancourt set out the principles underlying his new method. He advocated censorship, additions, modifications or modernization of the original text in the name of taste and linguistic and cultural differences. In addition, he expressed a desire to do more than merely translate: his objective was to create and polish a language that had by this time reached maturity. D'Ablancourt's translations did, in fact, hold a definite charm for their French readers.

VA: Yes, translations guided by the principles of a social class that ordered its life according to the concepts of *honnêteté* and *bienséance*. In this type of translation the approach is determined by a social ethos of what is right and proper.

IS: Exactly, the translator's pen guided by decency and decorum. I'm convinced, however, that inside every translator there is a Perrot d'Ablancourt eager to be recognized.

VA: What do you mean?

IS: Translators have the impossible task of navigating between fidelity and beauty. Who is it that said that translators are like women—when they are loyal they aren't beautiful and when they are beautiful they aren't loyal?

VA: I want to talk about authors who faced adversity in tyrannical regimes. In *Giving Offense: Essays on Censorship*, J.M. Coetzee includes an essay called "Osip Mandelstam and the Stalin Ode." In it he states:

> To Stalin and those members of the apparatus concerned with surveillance of the literary intelligentsia, what mattered was that every writer should make public obeisance to the great man and thus have both his pride and his spirit broken; in what spirit the praise-songs were sung was immaterial, as was the question of whether they constituted good or bad literature, as long as they did not carry discernible traces of insincerity—that is to say, traces of disobedience or even mockery.

Coetzee, I think, is after an exquisite form of censorship.

IS: Mandelstam died from mistreatment in a labor camp in Siberia in 1938, although he tried to commit suicide prior to his incarceration. That was the choice faced by numerous other writers and intellectuals. Mandelstam was forced not only to make public obeisance to the Man of Steel, but also to compose "proletariat" poetry. Yet, he remained true for as long as he could endure. On dissent, he wrote: "Perhaps my whisper was already born before my lips." And, of Stalin, he said: "He thinks in bone and feels with his brow/And tries to recall his human form." Anna Akhmatova was a friend of Mandelstam. She was also close to Boris Pasternak, a poet and the author of *Doctor*

Zhivago, another victim of state repression. Pasternak was awarded the Nobel Prize for literature in 1958, but the Soviet government didn't allow him to travel to Stockholm. Akhmatova composed several poems on Pasternak. In one of them, "Death of a Poet," she makes his passing in 1960 a cosmic rite of passage: "The unrepeatable voice won't speak again." She talks of how in death Pasternak reconnects with Nature (the harvest, the rain, the flowers) and how the whole planet, which bears "a name so modest... Earth," is now quiet as a result of his death.

Akhmatova has another astonishing poem about resistance and exile in which she is ready to assume the condition of exile: proud, disjointed, tearful. "We know there'll be a reckoning," she states, "an account for every hour." Joseph Brodsky was a pupil of hers, the one who chose—or was chosen by—exile.

VA: You met Brodsky in 1991.

IS: Yes, although we never talked about censorship. To me one of the most paradigmatic cases in the annals of Soviet literature is that of Isaac Babel.

VA: You wrote the introduction to the Spanish edition of *Odessa Stories* and *Red Cavalry* for the Mexican publisher Editorial Porrúa. The essay appears in English in *The Inveterate Dreamer*.

IS: I'm quite fond of that essay: "Isaac Babel: Tales of Ambivalence." Babel, as you know, was a Jew who wrote in the manner of Guy de Maupassant. His stories of Cossacks allow us to understand the inferiority complex by the hyper-intellectualized Odessa Jews toward those who excelled at physical labor. Babel was at first a favorite child of the Soviet regime and a Maxim Gorki protégé. But as time went by—and as his Jewish identity became more overt—he fell out of favor. He was pushed to a form of silence, which, in a writer like him, constitutes a substitute for suicide. In 1934, he gave an apology *pro vita sua* in the First Congress of the Union of Soviet Writers in Moscow. This, in my eyes, is one of the most memorable speeches ever delivered, especially given the ostracism the author was experiencing at the time. This was the era of "social realism," the proletarian approach to the novel endorsing class consciousness as the ultimate message for a writer to inject. He championed "the mediocre writer" in his speech (an allusion to Stalin's own literary efforts, no doubt). Babel stated:

> Some readers naively make a demand: "All right, describe me." And the writer thinks: "All right, I'll give him that description and make it true and honest." But that won't do. Into a description of Ivan Ivanovich there must be injected a philosophical view, some lofty ideas. For without out ideas, there can be no literature.

Having composed some of the best stories in the Russian language during the Soviet transformation, Babel became a writer of silence, one without a language of his own. Isn't this ironic, given his last name? As a Jew and a committed endorser of freedom, he was sacrificed at the stake of history, turned mute by the apparatchiks around him, a victim of twentieth-century obscurantism. Communism was meant to be a utopian landscape where everyone would be equal. Except that polysemy characterizes the language of ideology—and meanings become deliberately muddled. Communism undoubtedly tampered with the semantics of the term "equality."

VA: It most certainly did. In George Steiner's terms borrowing from the Bard: The language of ideology is full of sound and fury signifying nothing. As for the totalitarian meaning of "equality," Orwell said it best: "All animals are equal, but some animals are more equal than others." Let's now talk about another martyr of censorship in a despotic regime, Federico García Lorca, assassinated by an anonymous bullet in 1936, the first year of the Spanish Civil War.

IS: In *Residence on Earth*, Pablo Neruda included an ode to García Lorca. "By yourself you already know many things," he writes of his friend, "and others you will slowly get to know."

I've never been a fan of García Lorca. He strikes me as a mannerist poet who abused folklore for his own selfish purposes. His plays are unsatisfying to me: they feel contrived. Borges, not arbitrarily, once called him "a professional Andalusian."

VA: Let's go back for a bit to George Steiner. He is among the scholars whose work on translation has received the most attention. You have an essay on Steiner's memoir, *Errata*, in *The Inveterate Dreamer*. But I've never heard you say anything about *After Babel*.

IS: Steiner, I get the feeling, has a patrician attitude. He looks down at his readers as unworthy of his intellectual caliber. I used to read him with some regularity in *Salmagundi* and *The New Yorker,* but over time I've found far better ways to entertain my mind. Proof of my disdain is what happened to me some months ago, when I stumbled upon one of Steiner's essays, "On Difficulty," originally published in 1978. It opened with this sentence: "What do we mean when we say: 'this poem, or this passage in this poem is difficult'?" His response, unfortunately, was lacking.

> There is an obvious, crucial level at which this is a question about language itself. What is signified by the pragmatic experience that a lexically constituted and grammatically organized semantic system can generate impenetrability and undecidabilities of sense? No coherent answer can be given outside a complete model, such as we do not have, of the relations between "thought" and speech, and outside a total epistemology, which again we do not have, of the congruence or non-congruence of speech-forms with a "precedent" body of intention, perception, and vocative impulse. In such a model "difficulty" would, presumably, be an interference-effect between underlying clarity and obstructed formulation. This, roughly, is the classical and Cartesian reading of opaqueness, a reading whose inference is necessarily negative. But all the relevant terms—"inside"/"outside," "intentionality"/"verbalization," and the crucial "between" with its innocent postulate of a kind of mental space—are notoriously elusive. They activate a metaphor of separation

and transfer about which neither logic nor psychology are in any agreement.

"Undecidabilities"—ay, caramba! The paragraph proves to me the expectations Steiner sets for himself and his accomplishment. An essay reflecting on length as an excess in literature needs, by definition, to be short. Likewise, one on difficulty calls for simplicity of thought. But Steiner is a show-off. His objective isn't only to parade his semantic talent. He also wants us to feel that, unlike most of us, he *gets* a poem, even when it is difficult. For me the experience of literature is the experience of dialogue and not a competition by superior talents. Steiner suffers from the same malaise of academic "discourse." By building stylistic barriers impossible to sort by the lay reader, they put forth another form of self-censorship. Some would describe that form as Darwinian: you choose your own audience. But by doing so in such narrow a way, aren't you also curtailing your own message? That said, it would be preposterous to ignore Steiner's groundbreaking studies on language, included in *After Babel: Aspects of Language and Translation*. I read it in my youth in the Spanish translation published in Mexico by Fondo de Cultura Económica. It became a springboard from which I jumped to other seminal works, such as those by Ferdinand de Saussure.

VA: In *Ilan Stavans: Eight Conversations* with Neal Sokol, you've expressed enormous admiration for the British philosopher Isaiah Berlin. How does Berlin view censorship?

IS: Berlin is the opposite of Steiner and closer in spirit to Edmund Wilson, although one with a dramatically different approach to the marketplace of ideas. More than anything, he is a lucid interpreter of the Enlightenment. As we have talked about in earlier conversations, Berlin made a distinction between negative and positive freedom, and explained the difference between freedom and liberty in rousing ways. His views on censorship are easily summarized and follow along the lines of our conversations. Freedom doesn't mean the capacity to do and say anything one wishes. Civil society is built on respect and tolerance. These two concepts are based on self-imposed individual limitations. I don't desecrate the Qur'an, for instance, out of respect for the Islamic faith, but also because the same tolerance applies to me: I wouldn't want any book I hold sacred to be desecrated. Of course, this approach is summed up in the famous anecdote about Hillel, the rabbinical exegete. Once a stranger came to him and asked: "Rabbi, can you summarize the essence of Judaism while standing on one foot?" He smiled, stood on one leg, and answered: "Don't do onto others what you don't want done to you. The rest is commentary..." The famous fatwa against Salman Rushdie for publishing his novel *The Satanic Verses* is a useful example. Thousands in the Islamic world considered the book blasphemous (even though few ever actually read it). Its crime: Rushdie's "ridiculing" the life of Muhammad. Was Rushdie in his right to write such a fictional account? Of course, everyone is free to do as he wishes. Was he insensitive? No doubt. Did he deserve the punishment (years in hiding and under British police protection)? The answer is complicated. He had breached a tacit civil contract: he had offended the faithful. Furthermore, he had forgotten that East and West don't live under the same value system, that the concepts of freedom and tolerance in one are not the same in the other. Simply put, the Islamic world didn't go through an Enlightenment period. Berlin at Oxford said thus in the 1960s. He taught us that freedom is impossible in a society without economic security, a balanced health, and an embrace of open-minded knowledge. For freedom to exist, people need justice and equality. A limited degree of self-censorship is needed to establish tolerance and respect. He also taught us, though, that in theocracies people may have economic, physical, and material stability, but aren't free. I remember him making a reference once to the section on the Grand Inquisitor in Dostoyevsky's *The Brothers Karamzov* to show that paternalism might set the proper conditions for people to be free, yet also withhold the possibility of being free.

VA: What are your thoughts on censorship as it relates to Octavio Paz?

IS: I expounded a bit about it in my book *Octavio Paz: A Meditation*. Paz was a figure with a double-edge. He promoted intellectual and artistic freedom in Mexico from the end of World War II onward. His support for political freedom was a messier affair. He denounced the student massacre in Tlatelolco in 1968 by resigning from a diplomatic post he held. But as time went by, he became a puppet of the ruling party, the Partido Revolucionario

Institucional (PRI). In his monthly *Vuelta* he assembled free-thinkers from around the world, and he often wrote essays and poetry on freedom. Yet he became a Reaganite of sorts. At the end of his life, his conservative views made him a dinosaur, a man of letters disconnected from his own native soil.

VA: Is the vise of censorship positive for literature?

IS: It certainly can be. In *On Liberty,* John Stuart Mill argued that society isn't the one in needs to be protected from the wayward individual, but the individual whose rights need to be protected not only from what he terms the "tyranny of the magistrate," but from the "tyranny of the prevailing opinion and feeling." And Nadine Gordimer states that a writer's freedom "is his right to maintain and publish to the world a deep, intense, private view of the situation in which he finds his society. If he is to work as well as he can, he must take, and be granted, freedom from the public conformity of political inter-pretation, morals and tastes." When censorship, I add, is an obstacle, risking one's life is a worthy deed. Still, there are ways around censorship. Often those ways end up producing extraordinary literature. It is unpleasant to confess it but tyranny is good for literature. It gives writ-ers a raison d'être. The best asset I might identify on the impact of censorship on literature has to do with subtlety. Censorship is the engine that gives place to metaphor. In fact, I would go as far as to suggest that censoring regimes encourage baroque literature, for the baroque is the style indulging in tricks, ploys, side turns, and subterfuges.

VA: Then we could argue that even when censorship mobilizes a writer or translator to use devices for bypassing censorship, that in time these hypersubtle forms, as Coetzee has labeled them—born out of the game between the writer and his censor—themselves become conventions. So the secret language becomes even more subtle, and the meaning more obscure, and on and on until literature loses all traces of life.

IS: If that were to happen, the censors would be declared the winners. Authors aren't that stupid. Even in times of trouble, they don't write in order to conceal but to reveal. Metaphors, like adjectives, need to be used with caution. An abundance of them is a sign of bad writing.

VA: In the same line of thought, couldn't we argue that censorship is most useful to writers in the sense that they can capitalize on the restrictions and present themselves as an embattled tribe outnumbered by a Goliath?

IS: Yes, but is it good for writers to portray themselves as victims? Look at ethnic literature in the United States. It often takes the guise of activism, but it is often superficial, contrite, and predictable. Literature and politics have always had a troubled marriage. They easily contaminate each other. What's the proper balance? One of respect, but also distance.

VA: In one of the conversations you had with Neal Sokol, you state: "one must demand the impossible from translators." And in *Dictionary Days* you devote an entire essay to the word "impossible," arguing that it means "that which cannot be done." You suggest that lexicographers have left out the impossible from the lexicons they've done over the centuries.

IS: The impossible is beyond censorship.

VA: Of the many voices who have eloquently spoken on censorship, perhaps none is as sharp as Voltaire's. As a fellow lover of dictionaries, Ilan, let me offer you this quote from his *Dictionnaire Philosophique* of 1764 as closure to this conversation: "We have a natural right to make use of our pens as of our tongue, at our peril, risk, and hazard."

INDEX

Printed in the United States
By Bookmasters